The Secretary's

Software Survival Guide

Also available from Cassell:

The Professional Secretary John Spencer and Adrian Pruss
Volume 1: Communication Skills
Volume 2: Management Skills

Effective Communication for Managers Chris Simons and Belinda Naylor-Stables

Informative Writing, 2nd Edition Ken Goddard

An Introduction to Office Management for Secretaries Désirée Cox

An Introduction to Information Technology Anna Treby

Career Skills Patrick Forsyth

The Secretary's

Software Survival Guide

Deborah Knight

ORCA BOOK SERVICES

CASSELL

Cassell
Wellington House
125 Strand
London WC2R OBB

370 Lexington Avenue
New York, NY 10017-6550

www.cassell.co.uk

British Library Cataloguing-in-Publication Data
A catalogue record for this book is available from the British Library

ISBN 0-304-70350-8

First published 1998

Disclaimer

Because the author has no control over the circumstances of use of this
workbook, she cannot assume liability or responsibility for any consequential
loss or damage, however caused, arising as a result of carrying out the
instructions in this workbook. These materials are offered to the purchaser on
the basis of this understanding.

All of the information in the workbook is believed to be correct at the time of
printing. Whenever possible the author will try to assist with any queries.

Typeset using Microsoft Word for Windows by Deborah Kay Knight
Printed and bound in Great Britain by Redwood Books, Trowbridge, Wiltshire

Contents

Acknowledgements

I would like to thank
Stephen Power and David Knight
for their help and support.

Chapter One

How to Use this Book

Terminology

Clicking the Mouse

Most of the commands in this book require you to move the mouse pointer onto an item on the screen and then *click* it.

To *click* an item with the mouse simply hover over the required item, then press the *left-hand* mouse button.

Click and Drag

Occasionally you will be asked to click and drag over an area. To do this hold the left hand mouse button down, and move the mouse over the required area.

The Close Cross

The close cross is used for closing things down. It is found on the top right hand corner of packages, documents, dialogue boxes and message boxes.

When you are required to click on it you will be given the following command:-

Close **X**

Launching Packages

Before you can use any of the packages in this book you will need to launch them. Most packages that run on Windows 95 can be accessed via the *Start* button in the bottom left hand corner of the screen.

Sometimes shortcuts can be found on the first screen that comes up when Windows is loaded.

Menus and Buttons

Selecting Menu Items

All of the packages in this book have a menu bar. When you click on an item in the menu a sub menu will appear.

Fig 1.1 - A Submenu.

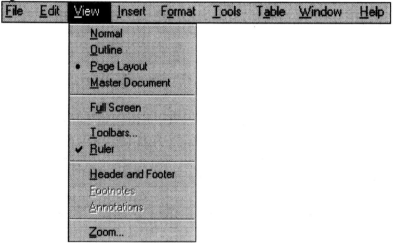

When you are required to click on an item in either the menu or sub menu it will appear in the instructions in bold type. For example:-

Click **View**
Click **Zoom**

The Button Bars

All of the packages contain buttons/icons on the screen. When you are required to click one it will be shown.

Using the Keyboard

When you need to press a key on the keyboard it will be shown in brackets.
For example:- **<Enter>**

Sometimes you will have to use two keys at once. Hold down the first key
that is shown and then press the second one.

For example:- **<Alt>** and **<Tab>**

Fig 1.2 - The Keyboard.

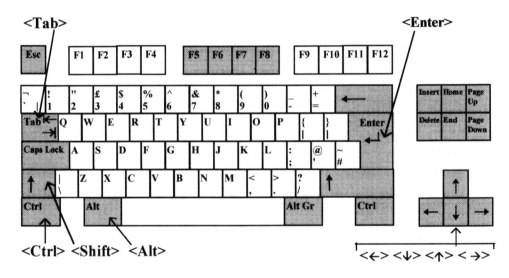

<Tab>   **<Enter>**

<Ctrl> <Shift> <Alt>   **<←> <↓> <↑> <→>**

Chapter Two

Microsoft® Access® for Windows®

This chapter was written for version 97, however in the main the
instructions are compatible with versions 2 and 7.

Getting Started

What is Microsoft Access?

Microsoft Access is used for creating databases. Databases are used to record information such as the details of all your customers or suppliers. Reports and queries can be created to pull out selected data.

Screen Layout

The *Menu Bar* appears at the top of the screen.

In addition to the menu there are various *buttons* on the screen, the buttons change when you enter different areas of Access.

Once you have created your first database file (see the following page) the *Database Window* is displayed on the screen. This displays a number of tags across the top. When you click on a tag, the section that it represents will jump to the front.

Figure 2.1 - The *Database Window*.

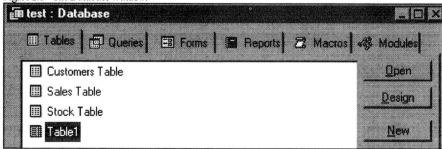

Files

Database Files

Microsoft Access uses files in the same way as any other package. However, you are prompted to give your file a name when you first create it. Another important factor is that the data that you key into the database is saved as soon as each item is entered, not when you close the file.

Creating a New File

1) Launch Microsoft Access.
   Select **Blank Database**.
   Click **OK**.

2) Type a name for it in the **File Name** box.
   Click **Create**.

Creating New Files after Access Has Been Launched

1) Click **File**.
   Click **New Database**.

2) Click the **General** tag.
   Click **Blank Database**.
   Click **OK**.

3) Type a name for it in the **File Name** box.
   Click **Create**.

Closing Files

To close a database file click the *Close* **X** in the top right hand corner of the *Database Window*.

Opening Existing Files

Opening a File

1)   Click **File**.
     Click **Open**.
     Alternatively, you can launch Microsoft Access and choose **More Files** at the first screen.

2)   Look at the list of files for the file that you are trying to open, and click on it. (If it is not in there then you may need to refer to the section below on 'Opening a File from Another Drive or Folder'.)

3)   Click **Open**.

Drives and Folders

For help in understanding the structure of drives and folders see Chapters 5 and 9 before following the instructions below.

Opening a File from Another Drive or Folder

1)   Click **File**, Click **Open**.

2)   If the File is on another drive then click the drop down arrow to the right of the **Look in** box, double click on the drive you need.

     If you can see your File at this point click on it, then click **Open**.

3)   To see the contents of a folder double click on it in the **Look in** box. A single folder may contain other folders, double click on these to view their contents.

4)   Once you have found your File, click on it.

5)   Click **Open**.

Tables

What are Tables?

A table is a grid of information. Each box in the grid is called a *field*. A row of fields is called a *record*. The heading at the top of each column is a *Field Name*.

Figure 2.2 - A table.

ID	Company	Town	County
1	Longleys Glass	Crawley	Sussex
2	Browns Repairs	Hove	Sussex
3	Shorts Shoes	Brighton	Sussex

Creating a Table

1) Make sure that the **Tables** tag is on top in the Database Window.

2) Click the **New** button, Click **Design View**, Click **OK.**

3) Type the name of your first field in **Field Name**, e.g. COMPANY.

4) Click the mouse in Data Type and an arrow will appear. Click on the arrow and choose a data type for your field. If the field is to contain text choose **text**, if it is to contain a number choose **number**.

5) Type a description in the description box - this is optional.

6) Repeat steps 3 - 5 for each field required.

Figure 2.3 - Designing a table.

Field Name	Data Type	Description
Company	Text	For names of companies
Town	Text	Part of company address
County	Text	Part of address

7) Click the *Close* **X** in the top right hand corner of the 'Create Table' window. Click **Yes** to save the table.

8) Name the table and click **OK**. You will be asked if you want a primary key, click **Yes**. This will provide each record with its own unique number.

Using the Table

Opening the Table

To view and use the table that you have created, select it from the database window and click the **Open** button. You will see an additional field called **ID**. This field will automatically provide each record with a unique number.

Figure 2.4 - An empty table.

ID	Company	Town	County

Entering Information

1) Use the <**Tab**> Key on the keyboard to take you from one box to another. Use <**Shift**>**and**<**Tab**> to take you back.

2) When you have finished entering information, click the *Close* **X** .

Finding Information

1) Click **Edit**, Click **Find**.

2) In **Find What**, type the information that you are looking for. This could be a word, a number or a combination of both.

3) If the text that you are searching for does not make up a whole field, select **Any Part of Field** in the **Match** box.

4) Click **Find First**. Click **Find Next** to find each subsequent occurrence.

Changing the Structure of a Table

1) Select your table from the Database Window.

2) Click the **Design** button.

Query Design

What is a Query?

Once you have keyed some data into your table you can *query* it to pull out sets of information. For example, you may want a list of all of the customers in Brighton.

Creating a Query

1) Click the **Queries** tag in the *database window*, click **New**. Click **Design View**. Click **OK**.

2) Select the table you are querying, click **Add**. Click **Close**. A grid will appear.

Figure 2.5 - Grid for preparing queries.

Field:			
Sort:			
Show:	☐	☐	☐
Criteria:			
or:			

3) In the first column of the table, click the *down arrow* on the **Field** box. A list of the fields in your table will appear. Select the first field that you require. Repeat this step for each field you need in the subsequent columns.

4) Input the information that you want to search for in the **Criteria** line, underneath the appropriate field name.

Figure 2.6 - Query to find all companies in Brighton.

Field:	Company	Town	County
Sort:			
Show:	☐	☐	☐
Criteria:		"Brighton"	
or:			

5) Click the *Close* **X** to close the query, click **Yes** to save changes. Click **OK**.

6) To view your query, select the query you want to see, click the **Open** button.

Queries on Numbers

Explanation

You way want to create some queries that use mathematical operators. For example, you might want to pick out all customers who have ordered over 200 items.

Use an Appropriate Table

You can only create a query that involves numbers if the field that you are querying on is a Number data type. Make sure that you select Number from the Data type box when you are creating your original table. Key some information into the table.

Figure 2.7 - Create a table that includes a numeric data type.

Field Name	Data Type	Description
Company	Text	For names of companies
Quantity	Number	Quantity of goods ordered

Designing the Query

Start to design the query in the normal way. Put the criteria that you wish to query the data by in the **Criteria row**, underneath the appropriate heading. In the following example, >200 has been keyed into the Quantity row, therefore the query will pull out all of the customers who have ordered more than 200 items.

Figure 2.8 - Query to show all customers who have ordered over 200 items.

Field:	Company	Quantity	
Sort:			
Show:	☐	☐	☐
Criteria:		>200	
or:			

>200	will pull out everybody who has ordered over 200 items
<200	will pull out everybody who has ordered less than 200 items
=200	will pull out everybody who has ordered exactly 200 items
>=200	will pull out everybody who has ordered 200 items and over.

Calculations in Queries

1) Create a table with some fields which are of the NUMBER data type.

Figure 2.9 - Design a table that includes numeric data types.

Field Name	Data Type
Company	Text
Price	Number
Quantity	Number

2) Key the applicable information into it.

ID	Company	Price	Quantity
1	Smith Ltd	34	8
2	Jones Ltd	12	6

3) Create a new query basing it on your table, select the fields that you require in the **Field** row of the grid.

4) In the next **Field** slot, type your calculation, as shown in Figure 2.10.

Figure 2.10 - A calculation in a query.

Field:	Company	Price	Quantity	=[Price]*[Quantity]
Sort:				
Show:	☒	☒	☒	☒
Criteria:				
or:				

5) Here are some examples of calculations that you could use.

=[Price]*[Quantity] This multiplies the fields Price and Quantity together
=[Price]+[Delivery] This adds the fields Price and Delivery together
=[Items]/[Staff]   This divides the field called Items by Staff
=[Amount]-[Tax]   This deducts the field called Tax from Amount.

6) Close down the query and open it to display the calculations.

Creating a Form

What is a Form?

Instead of entering information directly into the table, you can use a form. Only one record is displayed at a time so it can be easier to use.

Figure 2.11 - A table and a form.

ID	Company	Town	County
1	Longleys Glass	Crawley	Sussex
2	Browns Repairs	Hove	Sussex
3	Shorts Shoes	Brighton	Sussex

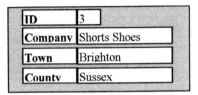

Creating a Form

1) Ensure that you have already created a table with the relevant fields.

2) Click the **Form** tag in the Database Window, click the **New** button.

3) Click the arrow next to **Choose the table or query where the objects data comes from** and select the table that you want to base your form on.

4) Select **Design View**, click **OK**.

   Click the *Field List* icon and a box with your fields with it will appear on the screen. If it is already on the screen, then the button will make it disappear.

Figure 2.12 - The *Field List* button and list.

 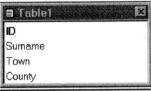

5) Click and drag the field names out of the box and onto the form.

6) Click the *Close* **X** to close the form. Click **Yes** to save the changes. Give it a name and click **OK**.

7) To use the form, select it from the Database Window, click the **Open** button.

Changing the Form

Making Changes

To make changes to the design of your form, select it from the main Access window. Click on the **Design** Button.

Moving and Resizing Fields

You may wish to alter the position or size of the fields on your form.

1) Single click on the field. A number of dots will appear around it.

2) The following diagram gives instructions on how to move and resize.

Figure 2.13 - Moving and resizing fields.

Use these dots to resize.

To move the field, click and drag on its border.

Use these bigger dots to move the field or label on its own.

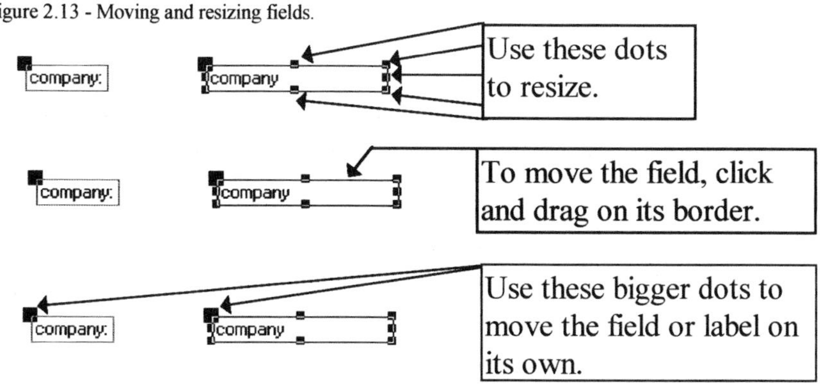

Enhancements

Select a field and the click one of the following:

This will change the background colour.

This will change the border width.

This changes the font colour.

This will give a field a special effect.

This changes the border colour.

Creating a Report

What is a Report?

Occasionally you may want to present your information in a more elaborate format than a table. You may also want to include calculations.

To Create a Report

1) Select the **Reports** tag from the *Database Window*, click the **New** button.

2) Select the table that you wish to base your report on. Do this by clicking the drop down arrow in the box labelled **Choose the table or query where the object data comes from**.

3) Select **Design View**. Click **OK**.

4) Click the *Field List* icon and a box with your fields in it will appear on the screen. If it is already on the screen, then the button will make it disappear.

Figure 2.14 - The *Field list* button and list.

 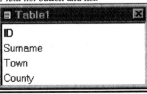

5) Click and drag the fields onto the report.

   For instructions on how to move and resize, see the section on moving and resizing fields in forms.

6) Click the *Close* **X** to close down the report. Click **Yes** to save the changes. Give it a name and click **OK**.

7) To see your report, select it from the *Database Window*, click the **Preview** button.

Calculations in Reports

1) Create a table that has some fields which are of a NUMBER type.

2) Create a new report.

3) Drag all the fields that you require onto the report. Make sure you include the number fields.

4) Click on the *Text Box* button, and then click and drag on the report to make an unbound field.

Figure 2.15 - The *Text Box* button makes an unbound field.

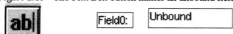

5) Click inside the Unbound box and type a calculation.

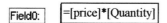

The example shown above would multiply the price and the quantity together. For examples of other calculations, see the section on calculations in queries.

6) Click in the label for the field and type a sensible heading. Keep the colon at the end of the heading.

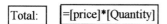

7) Click the *Close* **X** to close down the report. Click **Yes** to save the changes. Give it a name and click **OK**.

8) To see your report, select it from the *Database Window*. Click **Preview**.

Chapter Three

Lotus® Approach®

This chapter was written for Release 3, however in the main the instructions are compatible with the 97 Edition.

Getting Started

What is Approach?

Lotus Approach is used for creating databases. Databases are used to record information such as the details of all your customers or suppliers. The information can be interrogated in order to find records that meet a certain criteria.

Screen Layout

Once you have designed a database, the *Menu Bar* will be displayed on the screen.

In addition to the menu bar, various *Smart Icons* will be displayed.

Creating a New Database

1) Launch Lotus Approach.

2) Select **Create a new file**.

3) Click **OK**.

4) Give your database a name in **File name**.

5) Click **OK**.

Designing the Database

Setting up the Fields

1) You now need to define some *Fields*. Our example will use the following fields:-

COMPANY   (This will record company names.)
TOWN   (This will record the town they are based in.)
EMPLOYEES (This will record the number of employees they have.)

2) Enter the field name COMPANY in the **Field Name** box.

3) Each field needs a **Data Type**. For example the field called COMPANY will contain text so select **Text** in the **Data Type** box.

4) Text fields need a **Size** so enter the maximum number of characters that this field will contain in the **Size** box.

5) Repeat steps 2 - 4 to set up the TOWN and EMPLOYEES fields. *Employee* will be a **number** data type because it will house figures. When you have finished, click **OK**.

Figure 3.1 - Setting up fields.

Field Name	Data Type	Size	Formula / Options
Company	Text	25	
Town	Text	20	
Employees	Numeric	10.2	

Entering Information

Entering Information into a Form

1) Once you have set up the fields, an empty form will be displayed on the screen.

   Each set of blank fields is known as a *Record*.

Figure 3.2 - A data entry form.

Company	Town	Employees

Use the **<Tab>** key on the keyboard to jump from one field to another. Type the relevant information for each field in order to complete the first record.

Figure 3.3 - One record.

Company	Town	Employees
Bits and Bobs	Brighton	20

2) You may need to use this button on the button bar to bring up a new blank record.

3) Use these buttons to move between records.

Using the Worksheet

To display the information in a worksheet click the **Worksheet** tag at the top of the screen. Use **<Tab>** to move from field to field.

Figure 3.4 - Using the worksheet.

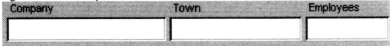
The Worksheet Tag

Company	Town	Employees
Bits and Bobs	Brighton	20
Colins Cables	Crawley	98
Sandy Bay Foods	Brighton	23
Heron Engineering	Crawley	120

Adding More Fields

Adding a New Field to an Existing Database

1) Click **Create**.

2) Click **Field Definition**.

    The screen where you can stipulate the fields that you need will appear.

3) Add the new field. In our example this is a field called COUNTY.

County	Text	10

4) Click **OK**.

    The form will now be displayed in *Design View*. An additional box will
    appear on the screen entitled **Add Field**.

    Figure 3.4 - Box containing the new field.

    Drag the name of your new field out of the box and onto the form using the
    mouse.

    After you have dragged the field onto the form, a box will pop up asking you if
    you wish to *Design* or *Browse*. Click **Design**.

5) When you are satisfied with the position of the field, click **View**, click **Browse**.

Finding Sets of Records

1) Click on the Worksheet Tag.

2) Click on the button shown below.

A grid will be displayed.

Figure 3.6 - Grid used for finding information.

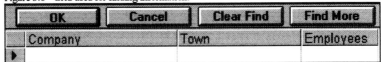

3) Enter the criterion that you wish to search for in the field in which it appears in your database. The following example shows how you would pull out all the companies in Brighton.

Figure 3.7 - Setting the criterion to find all companies in Brighton.

Company	Town	Employees
	Brighton	

4) Click **OK**.

5) You will now see a list of all the companies in Brighton.

Company	Town	Employees
Bits and Bobs	Brighton	20
Sandy Bay Foods	Brighton	23

6) To display all the records again, click the following button.

Finding Records that Match Numerical Criteria

1) Bring up the *Find* grid in the normal way.

2) In our example we shall find all companies that have over 20 employees, so click in the Employee Column.

Click the *greater than* Button.

Enter a figure, in our example 20.

Figure 3.8 - Set the criterion to find companies with more than 20 employees.

Company	Town	Employees
▶		>20

3) Click **OK**.

You should now see a list of all companies that employ over 20 people.

Figure 3.9 - Records where the number of employees is greater than 20.

Company	Town	Employees
Colins Cables	Crawley	98
Sandy Bay Foods	Brighton	23
Heron Engineering	Crawley	120

4) You can make up criteria using the following symbols and the appropriate figures.

Figure 3.10 - Some sample queries.

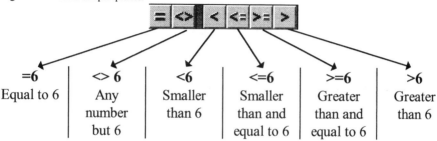

=6	<> 6	<6	<=6	>=6	>6
Equal to 6	Any number but 6	Smaller than 6	Smaller than and equal to 6	Greater than and equal to 6	Greater than 6

Calculations

1) Create a database containing some fields with numerical data types.

Figure 3.11 Fields with numerical data types.

Field Name	Data Type	Size
Company	Text	10
Staff at Head Office	Numeric	10.2
Staff in Branches	Numeric	10.2
Total Staff	Numeric	10.2

2) Click on the field that is to contain the calculation.

3) Click **Options**.

4) Click **Creation Formula**.

5) A formula creation menu will appear. Click on the list of **Fields** and the list of **Operators** in order to create a formula. As you click on them, they will appear in the formula box at the bottom.

Figure 3.12 - Example formula.

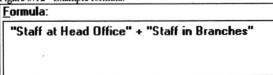

Formula:

"Staff at Head Office" + "Staff in Branches"

6) Click **OK** to come out of the formulas menu.

7) Click **OK** to finish creating the fields.

8) As you key the information into your database, the field with the formula associated with it will display a result.

Record Numbers

Clarification

It is good database practice to give each record a unique number by which it can be identified. You cannot rely on any of the other fields in order to isolate a record.

Creating Record Numbers

1) Create a field for the record number. Give it a *Numeric* **Data Type**.

Figure 3.13 - A field with a numeric data type.

Field Name	Data Type	Size
Reference Number	Numeric	10.2

2) Click **Options**.

3) Click **Serial Number Starting at**.
   Click **Validation**. Click **Unique**.
   The formula options box associated with the field will now read Auto-enter Serial.

4) Create the rest of the fields as normal.

Figure 3.14 Prepare the rest of the fields.

Field Name	Data Type	Size
Reference Number	Numeric	10.2
Company	Text	10
Staff at Head Office	Numeric	10.2
Staff in Branches	Numeric	10.2
Total Staff	Numeric	10.2

5) The *Record Number* field will automatically provide you with the next sequential number whenever you enter a new record.

Opening an Existing Database

Opening a Database

1) Click **File**.
   Click **Open**.

2) Look at the list of files for the file that you are trying to open, and click on it. (If it is not in there then you may need to refer to the section below on 'Opening a File in Another Drive or Directory'.)

3) Click **OK**.

Drives and Directories

For help in understanding the structure of drives and directories, see Chapter 6 before following the instructions below.

Opening a File in Another Drive or Directory

1) Click **File**, Click **Open**.

2) If the document is on another drive then click the drop down arrow to the right of the **Drives** box, click on the drive that you need.

   If you can see your document at this point click on it, then click **OK**.

3) To see the contents of a folder, double click on it in the **Directories** box. A single folder may contain other folders, double click on these to view their contents.

4) Once you have found your document, click on it.

5) Click **OK**.

Chapter Four

Microsoft® Excel® for Windows®

This chapter was written for version 97, however in the main the instructions are compatible with versions 5 and 7.

Introduction

What is Microsoft Excel?

Microsoft Excel is a Spreadsheet Package. It is used for storing numerical information. It can be used for recording sales figures, accounting, petty cash or any task which involves calculations.

Workbooks

Each file in Excel is known as a *Workbook*.

Screen Layout

The *Menu Bar* appears at the top of the screen.

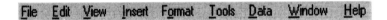

In addition to the menu bar there are various *Buttons* on the screen.

Rows, Columns and Cells

The workbooks in Excel are made up of *Rows* and *Columns*. Each *Column* is referenced by a letter. Each *Row* is referenced by a number. Each *Cell* has a unique cell reference depending on which *Column* and which *Row* it is in. For example if the cursor is in *Column* A, *Row* 3, then it is in *Cell* A3.

Figure 4.1 - Cells.

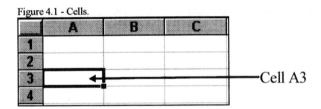

—Cell A3

Moving from Cell to Cell

Either:
1) Use the arrow keys on the keyboard <←> <→> <↑> <↓>, or
2) Press <**Enter**> to go down one cell at a time, or
3) Click the mouse in the cell that you wish to move to.

Entering Information into a Cell

1) Type the information into the appropriate cell.
2) Always move out of the cell in order for the information to be recorded.

Sheets

There are several sheets in each Excel File. Each sheet can be used for a different purpose. For example, Sheet1 could be used for expenses, and Sheet2 for petty cash. To get to each sheet, single click on the sheet tags at the bottom of the screen.

Figure 4..2 - The sheet tags.

| ◄ | ► | ◄| | |►| **Sheet1** / Sheet2 / Sheet3 /

Renaming a Sheet

To re-name a sheet tag, double click on the tag.

Creating a New Workbook

Microsoft Excel provides you with a blank workbook to type on when you launch the program. When you need another new document click the *New* icon, shown below.

Saving Workbooks

Saving and Naming a Workbook

The first time that you save a Workbook, you need to give it a name.

1) Click **File**.
2) Click **Save As**.
3) Type a Name for the Workbook in **File name**.
4) Click **Save**.

Saving the Changes to a Workbook

Once you have saved the workbook for the first time and named it, you may need to make changes to it and re-save it. Use the following method for this.

1) Click **File**.
2) Click **Save**.

Using the Buttons

Click this button instead of **Save** or **Save As**.

The first time that you click the *save* button in each workbook the *Save As* screen will appear so that you can name it. When you click this button after the worksheet has been named, the changes will be saved.

Opening Workbooks

Opening a Workbook

1) Click **File**.
   Click **Open**.

2) Look at the list of files for the file that you are trying to open, and click on it.
   (If it is not in there, you may need to refer to the section below on 'Opening a
   Workbook in Another Drive or Folder'.)

3) Click **Open**.

Drives and Folders

For help in understanding the structure of drives and folders, see Chapters 5
and 9 before following the instructions below.

Opening a Workbook in Another Drive or Folder

1) Click **File**, click **Open**.

2) If the Workbook is on another drive then click the drop down arrow to the right
   of the **Look in** box, double click on the drive you need.

   Look for your name of your workbook, click on it, then click **Open**.

3) To see the contents of a folder, double click on it in the **Look in** box. A single
   folder may contain other folders, double click on these to view their contents.

4) Once you have found your Workbook click on it, then click **Open**.

Formulas

Entering a Formula

The primary purpose of the spreadsheet is to perform calculations. Each one of these calculations is known as a formula.

1) Go to the cell where you wish the formula to appear.
2) Type in the formula (see simple formulas below).
3) Press the ENTER Key and the answer will appear in the cell.

Simple Formulas

Adding

=A1+A2   This will add the amount in cell A1 to the amount in cell A2.

Subtracting

=A1-A2   This will subtract the amount in A2 from the amount in A1.

Multiplying

=A1*A2   This will multiply the amount in A1 by the amount in A2.

Dividing

=A1/A2   This will divide the amount in A1 by the amount in A2.

Figure 4.3 - Using formulas.

	A	B	C	D	E
1	2	5	5	8	
2	4	2	2	2	
3	=A1+A2	=B1-B2	=C1*B2	=D1/D2	

Totalling Columns

Using the Keyboard

1) Type a column of numbers.

2) Go to the cell in which the total is to appear (in our example A6).
   Type the following formula:
   =SUM(A1:A5)

   A1 and A5 are the first and last cells of the range to be added.

Figure 4.4 - Totalling a column of figures.

	A	B	C	D
1	44			
2	334			
3	523			
4	745			
5	26			
6	=SUM(A1:A5)			

3) Press <**Enter**> and the total will appear.

6	1672			

Using the Autosum Button

1) Type a column of numbers. Click in the cell in which the total is to appear (in our example A6).

2) Click the autosum button, the formula will appear in the cell.

6	=SUM(A1:A5)			

3) Check that the range to be added is shown in the brackets (if it is not, then click and drag the mouse over the required area), press <**Enter**>. The total appears.

6	1672			

Copying Formulas

Copying Formulas Across Columns

Once you have performed a calculation in the first column of a set of numbers you can copy the formula to each subsequent column.

1) Perform your calculation for the first column (in our example a total).

Figure 4.5 - Preparing to copy a formula.

	A	B	C	D
1	4	4	3	4
2	3	7	3	6
3	5	2	6	7
4	7	4	4	5
5	2	6	2	3
6	21			

Total

2) Click and drag the mouse over the total and the subsequent cells to the right.

Figure 4.1. - Selecting the cells to be filled.

	A	B	C	D
1	4	4	3	4
2	3	7	3	6
3	5	2	6	7
4	7	4	4	5
5	2	6	2	3
6	21			

Select these cells

3) Click **Edit**, click **Fill**, click **Right**.

Copying Formulas Down Rows

1) Total your first row.

2) Click and drag the mouse over the total and the subsequent cells below.

3) Click **Edit**, click **Fill**, click **Down**.

Copying and Moving Information

Copying Information

1) Select the cells to be copied with the mouse.
2) Click **Edit**, click **Copy**.
3) Click the mouse at the point where the copy must appear.
4) Click **Edit**, click **Paste**.

Moving Information

1) Select the cells to be moved with the mouse.
2) Click **Edit**, click **Cut**.
3) Click the cursor at the point where the information must reappear.
4) Click **Edit**, click **Paste**.

Using the Icons

1) Select the cells to be moved or copied with the mouse.

Use this button instead of **Edit** and **Cut**.   Use this button instead of **Edit** and **Copy**.

2) Click at the point where you want the information to appear.

Use this button instead of **Edit** and **Paste**.

Deleting

1) Drag the mouse over the cells to be emptied.
2) Click **Edit,** click **Cut,** or press the **<Delete>** key on the keyboard.

Moving or Copying Text to Other Files

Moving Text to Another File

1)   Open the File containing the information to be moved.
     Open the File where the information is to be copied to.

2)   Click **Window**.
     You should see your two open Files listed at the bottom of the Menu.
     Select the File containing the information to be moved.

3)   Select the information to be copied with the mouse.
     Click **Edit**, click **Cut**.

4)   Select **Window**.
     Select the File that the information is to be moved to.
     Click in the destination File at the point where you would like the copied
     information to appear.
     Click **Edit**,   click **Paste**.

Copying Text to Another File

1)   Open the File containing the information to be copied.
     Open the File where the information is to be copied to.

2)   Click **Window**.
     You should see your two open Files listed at the bottom of the Menu.
     Select the File containing the information to be copied.

3)   Select the information to be copied with the mouse.
     Click **Edit**, click **Copy**.

4)   Select **Window**.
     Select the File in which the copied information should appear.
     Click in the destination File at the point where you would like the copied
     information to appear.
     Click **Edit**,   click **Paste**.

Inserting and Deleting Rows and Columns

Inserting Rows

1) Click in the row underneath where you want the new row to appear.
2) Click **Insert**.
3) Click **Rows**.

Deleting Rows

1) Click in the row that you wish to delete.
2) Click **Edit**.
3) Click **Delete**.
4) Click **Entire row**.

Inserting Columns

1) Click to the right of where you want the new column to appear.
2) Click **Insert**.
3) Click **Columns**.

Deleting Columns

1) Click in the column that you wish to delete.
2) Click **Edit**.
3) Click **Delete**.
4) Click **Entire column**.

Printing

Printing a Sheet

1) Go to the sheet that you want to print.
2) Click **File**.
3) Click **Print**.
4) Click **Active Sheet(s)**.
5) Click **OK**.

Using the Icon

1) Click this icon.

2) One copy of all the pages in the current sheet will be sent to print.

Printing a Selection

1) Select cells to be printed with the mouse.
2) Click **File**.
3) Click **Print**.
4) Click **Selection.**
5) Click **OK**.

Printing the Whole Workbook

1) Click **File**.
2) Click **Print**.
3) Click **Entire workbook**.
4) Click **OK**.

Format of Cells

Changing the Font Size

1) Select the cells to be altered with the mouse.

2) Click the drop down arrow to the right of the following icon:
   `12` ⬇ When the list of sizes drops down you will see a scroll bar on the right hand side of the list - use this to scroll to other sizes.

3) Select the size you want by clicking on the actual number.

Changing the Font Style

1) Select the cells to be altered with the mouse.

2) Click the drop down arrow to the right of the following icon:
   `Times New Roman` ⬇ When the list of fonts drops down you will see a scroll bar on the right hand side of the list - use this to scroll to even more fonts.

3) Select the font you want by clicking on its name.

Bold, Italics and Underline

1) Select the cells to be altered with the mouse.

2) Select one or more of the following buttons:
   B Use for Bold   *I* Use for Italic   U Use for Underline

3) To take one of the enhancements off - simply select the area to be altered and click the button again. Occasionally you may have to click the same button twice if you have selected a mixed area.

Alignment of Cells

Changing the Alignment

Information can be arranged in the cells in three different ways:-

Figure 4.2. - Alignment of cells.

On the left	In the middle	On the right
Item One	9876	986
Item Two	98	98
Item Three	0987	987

1)   Select the cells to be altered with the mouse.

2)   Click this button to   Click this button to   Click this button to
      left-align cells.   centre the cells.   right-align the cells.

The Default

Unless you change the alignment of your cells, numbers will always align on the right hand side of the cells, and text will always align on the left hand side.

Figure 4.8 - Default alignment.

Site	Employees
Town Centre	23
Industrial Estate	124
Business Centre	34

Charts - I

Creating a Column Chart

1) Enter the categories and the relevant figures into a group of cells, placing the categories above the figures.

Figure 4.3. - Figures prepared for a chart.

London	Crawley	Hove	Brighton
600	500	200	300

2) Select all of the information with the mouse.

3) Click **Insert**, click **Chart**.

4) In **Chart Type**, select **Column**.

5) Click **Next**, click **Next** again.

6) Insert a **Chart title**, for example: SALES.

7) Insert a **Category (X) Axis**. For example: TOWNS.

8) Insert a **Value (Y) Axis**. For example: UNITS SOLD.

9) Click **As new sheet**, click **Finish**.

Figure 4.10 - Bar chart.

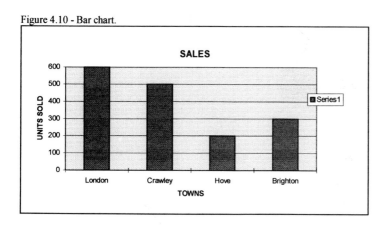

Charts - II

Creating a Pie Chart

1) Enter the categories and the relevant figures into a group of cells, placing the categories above the figures.

Figure 4.11 - Figures prepared for a chart.

London	Crawley	Hove	Brighton
600	500	200	300

2) Select all of the information with the mouse.

3) Click **Insert**, click **Chart**. In **Chart Type**, select **Pie**.

4) Click **Next**, click **Next** again.

5) Type a title in **Chart title**. For example: SALES.

6) Click the **Data Labels** tag. Click **Show label and percent**.

7) Click **Next**, click **As new sheet**.

8) Click **Finish**.

Figure 4.12 - Pie chart.

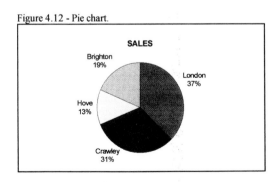

Chapter Five

Microsoft® Explorer®

This chapter was written for Windows 95®. However in the main the instructions are compatible with Windows 98®.

Getting Started

What is Explorer?

Explorer is a utility found on Windows 95 and Windows 98 for organising the information on your computer. There are facilities for creating directories, copying files, and moving files.

Launching Explorer

1) Click the *Start* Button on the *Task Bar* at the bottom of the computer screen.

2) Select **Programs**.

3) Select **Windows Explorer**.

The Layout of the Screen

Once you have launched Explorer, you will see two sets of information on either side of the computer screen. The tree on the left hand side shows the main categories. When you double click on one of these categories, the subsections within it are shown on the right hand side.

The example below shows the contents of both sides of the screen as a folder called *Company* is selected. The folder contains three letters, Let1, Let2 and Let3.

Figure 5.1 - Viewing the contents of a folder.

All Folders	Contents of 'Company'
Desktop	Name
My Computer	Let1
3½ Floppy (A:)	Let2
(C:)	Let3
Audio	
Balloon	
Company	

Major Categories

The Desktop

This section appears at the top of the tree. It contains the icons for all the drives and utilities on your computer. In some cases it shows the route to other networks.

My Computer

This section contains all of the drives and files within your computer.

The Drives

The [C:] drive is found within *My Computer*. It represents the hard drive that is inside your computer.

The [A:] drive is found within *My Computer*. It represents the small drive in front of your computer. This is the one that you put small floppy disks into.

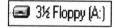

The [D:] drive is usually the CD-ROM drive.

Folders

These can be found on any drive of your computer. They contain files.

Creating Folders

Positioning

Firstly you need to decide where you would like your new folder to be placed.

If you want it to be directly on the **[C:]** drive then simply launch **Explorer** and double click on the **[C:]** icon in the left hand side of the screen.

If you want to position it *inside* an existing folder then you need to locate this folder, and double click on it to open it up.

Creating the Folder

1) Click **File**.

2) Select **New**.

3) Select **Folder**.

4) A new folder will now appear on the right hand side of the screen containing the words 'New Folder'. Click the mouse on the words 'New Folder' on this icon and rename it to suit you. Click just outside of the box containing the folder name.

Figure 5.2 - A new folder.

Deleting Files or Folders

Single click the mouse on the file or folder that you wish to delete. Alternatively put your hand on the **<Ctrl>** key of the keyboard and click on several files or folders. Press the **<Delete>** key on the keyboard.

Copying Files

Copying Files to a Floppy Disk

1)   Double click the [C:] icon.

2)   Double click the folder that contains the file/s to be copied.

3)   The files should be displayed on the right hand side of the screen. To select the files that you wish to copy, single click on them with the mouse. (To select more than one file press the <Ctrl> key on the keyboard and single click the additional files required.)

4)   Click **Edit**, click **Copy**.

5)   Ensure that you have a floppy disk in the drive. Double click on the [A:] icon.

6)   Click **Edit** , click **Paste**.

Copying Documents to Another Folder

1)   Double click the [C:] icon.

2)   Double click the folder that contains the file/s to be copied.

3)   The files should be displayed on the right hand side of the screen. To select the files that you wish to copy, single click on them with the mouse. (To select more than one file press the Ctrl key on the keyboard and single click the additional files required.)

4)   Click **Edit**, click **Copy**.

5)   Double click on the folder that you wish to copy the document to.

6)   Click **Edit**, click **Paste**.

Moving Files

Moving Files to a Floppy Disk

1) Double click the [C:] icon.

2) Double click the folder that contains the file/s to be moved.

3) The files should be displayed on the right hand side of the screen. To select the files that you wish to move, single click on them with the mouse. (To select more than one file press the <Ctrl> key on the keyboard and single click the additional files required.)

4) Click **Edit**, click **Cut**.

5) Ensure that you have a floppy disk in the drive. Double click on the [A:] icon.

6) Click **Edit** , click **Paste**.

Moving Documents to Another Folder

1) Double click the [C:] icon.

2) Double click the folder that contains the file/s to be copied.

3) The files should be displayed on the right hand side of the screen. To select the files that you wish to move, single click on them with the mouse. (To select more than one file press the Ctrl key on the keyboard and single click the additional files required.)

4) Click **Edit**, click **Cut**.

5) Double click on the folder that you wish to move the document to.

6) Click **Edit**, click **Paste**.

Chapter Six

Microsoft® File Manager®

This chapter was written for Windows® 3.11. However in the main the instructions are compatible with version 3.1.

Getting Started

What is File Manager?

The File Manager is a utility found on Windows 3.1 and Windows 3.11.

It is used for organising the information on your computer. There are facilities for creating directories, copying files, moving files and deleting files.

Launching File Manager

1)   Locate the File Manager icon shown below.

It should be in the *Main* program group in the *Program Manager*. The Program Manager is what you see when you first go into Windows.

File Manager

Figure 6.1 - The *File Manager* icon.

2)   Double click the **File Manager** icon.

Screen Layout

The *Menu Bar* appears at the top of the screen.

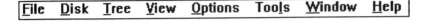

| File | Disk | Tree | View | Options | Tools | Window | Help |

In addition to the menu there are various *Buttons* on the screen.

Drives

The Drive Icons

Look for a bar at the top of the screen that depicts the drives.

Figure 6.2 - The drives.

To view the contents of a drive, double click on the relevant icon. A window will open displaying all the directories and files on the drive.

The Most Common Drives

1) The C Drive

The **C** drive is the Hard Drive located inside your computer. This contains all the files which enable your computer to run.

2) The A Drive

The **A** Drive is the small drive in front of your computer. This is the one that you put small floppy disks into.

3) The D Drive

This is usually the CD-ROM drive.

Directories

What are Directories?

The information on your drives needs to be organised. Directories are used to separate files into groups. Each directory is given a name that is relevant to the files that are contained within it.

Figure 6.3 - A directory.

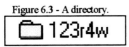

Directories are arranged in a tree structure, with the **C:** being known as the root directory. To view all of the main directories on your computer, double click the C:\ at the top of the directory tree on the left hand side of the screen. All of the main directories will appear on the right hand side of the screen.

Figure 6.4 - The root directory.

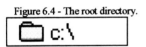

To see what you have got in a directory, double click on it. The example below shows a directory called 'company' on the left hand side. On the right hand side you can see the three files that are in it.

Figure 6.5 - A selected directory.

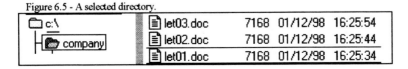

Sub-directories

A sub-directory is a directory within a directory. If you look at the example below you will see that the company directory contains another directory called 'accounts'.

Figure 6.6 - A sub-directory.

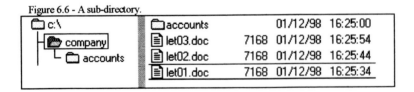

Creating Directories

Positioning the Directory

Firstly you need to decide where you would like your new directory to be placed.

If you want it to be directly on the **C:** drive, double click on the **C:** at the top of the directory tree.

If you want to position it *inside* an existing directory then you need to locate this directory, and double click on it to open it up.

Creating a Directory

1)   Click **File**.

2)   Select **Create Directory**.

3)   Give your directory a name.

4)   Click **OK**.

Copying Files

Copying Documents to a Floppy Disk

1)   Double click the directory that contains the document/s to be copied.

2)   Single click the document to be copied. (To select more than one file press the <Ctrl> key on the keyboard and single click the additional files required.)

3)   Click **File**, click **Copy**.

4)   In the **To** box type: **A:**

5)   Click **OK**.

Copying Documents to Another Folder

1)   Double click the directory that contains the document/s to be copied.

2)   Single click the document to be copied. (To select more than one file press the <Ctrl> key on the keyboard and single click the additional files required.)

3)   Click **File**, click **Copy**.

4)   In the **To** box, type the name of the drive and directory that the files are to be copied to.

For example:

C:\Company

This would copy all of the files to the company directory on the C drive.

5)   Click **OK**.

Moving Files

Moving Documents to a Floppy Disk

1) Double click the directory that contains the document/s to be moved.

2) Single click the document to be moved. (To select more than one file press the <Ctrl> key on the keyboard and single click the additional files required.)

3) Click **File**, click **Move**.

4) In the **To** box, type: **A:**

5) Click **OK**.

Moving Documents to Another Directory

1) Double click the directory that contains the document/s to be moved.

2) Single click the document to be copied. (To select more than one file press the <Ctrl> key on the keyboard and single click the additional files required.)

3) Click **File**, click **Move**.

4) In the **To** box, type the name of the drive and directory that the files are to be moved to.

   For example:

   C:\Company

   This would move all of the files to the company directory on the C drive.

5) Click **OK**.

Deleting Files

Deleting Files

1)   Double click the directory that contains the document/s to be deleted.

2)   Single click the document to be deleted. (To select more than one file press the <Ctrl> key on the keyboard and single click the additional files required.)

3)   Click **File**, click **Delete**.

Undelete

Some versions of Windows will allow you to undelete files should you accidentally remove them. However, the files do not stay in 'Undelete' forever, so be sure to use undelete as soon as you realise you need to restore something.

1)   Ensure that you are in the directory that you deleted the file from.

2)   Click **File**.

3)   Click **Undelete**.

4)   A list of the files that you can undelete will come up, this list will only show the files that have been deleted from the directory that you are in.

5)   Select the file that you wish to undelete.

6)   Click the **Undelete** Button.

7)   Replace the **?** with a letter (usually the first letter of the file you deleted).

8)   Click **OK**.

Floppy Disks

Formatting a Floppy Disk

Formatting a floppy disk will completely clear all of the information on it. It also prepares it for use in the computer.

1) Launch the File Manager.

2) Click **Disk**, click **Format Disk**.

3) Make sure that it says Drive A in the **Disk in** box.

4) Click **OK**.

5) Click **Yes** to confirm that you wish to format the disk.

6) The computer will now format the disk.

7) When it has finished you will be asked if you wish to format another disk. If you do not then click **No**.

Copying Disks

1) Launch File Manager.

2) Click **Disk**, click **Copy Disk**.

3) Click **Yes** to confirm that you want to continue.

4) You will be asked for the Source Disk. This is the disk to be copied. Insert it into the machine and click **OK**.

5) When it is half way through the process, you will be asked to insert the Destination Disk. This is the disk that will become the copy. Insert the Destination Disk. Click **OK**.

6) The information will now be written on to the second disk.

Chapter Seven

Lotus® Freelance Graphics®

This chapter was written for Release 2.1, however in the main the instructions are compatible with the 97 Edition.

Getting Started

What is Freelance Graphics?

Freelance Graphics is designed for the creation of presentations. These presentations can be in the form of acetates for an overhead projector. Alternatively, the slides can be projected directly onto a computer screen.

Creating the First Slide

1) Launch Freelance Graphics. Make sure **Create a New Presentation** is selected. Click **OK**.

2) Either choose a look for your presentation from the list, or click **Smartmaster with blank background**.

3) Select **Title** from the **Choose a layout for the current page** list, click **OK**.

4) You now have a blank slide on the screen. Click the labelled areas of the slide in order to add a title, subtitle or symbol.

Figure 7.1 - A blank slide.

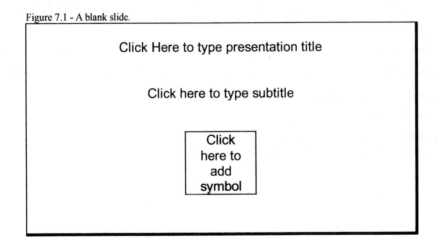

Working with Several Slides

Creating Another Slide

1) Click the **New Page** button at the bottom of the screen.

2) Select **Title** from the **Choose a layout for the current page** list, click **OK**.

Slide Sorter

1) Create several new slides.

2) Click on the Slide Sorter button.

3) All of your slides will now be displayed on the screen in miniature.

Figure 7..2 - Viewing the slides in the slide sorter.

4) Select the slide that you want to edit.

5) Click this button to view it on the screen.

Saving Presentations

Saving and Naming a Presentation

The first time that you save a presentation, you need to give it a name.

1)   Click **File**.
2)   Click **Save As**.
3)   Type a name for the presentation in **File name**.
4)   Click **OK**.

Saving the Changes to a Presentation

Once you have saved the presentation for the first time and named it, you may need to make changes to it and re-save it. Use the following method for this.

1)   Click **File**.
2)   Click **Save**.

Using the Buttons

Click this button instead
of **Save** or **Save As**.

The first time that you click the *save* button in each presentation, the *Save As* screen will appear so that you can name it. When you click this button after the worksheet has been named, the changes will be saved.

Opening Presentations

Opening a File

1) Click **File**.
   Click **Open**.

2) Look at the list of files underneath the **File name** box for the file that you are trying to open, and click on it.
   (If it is not in there then you may need to refer to the section below on 'Opening a File from Another Drive or Directory'.)

3) Click **OK**.

Drives and Directories

For help in understanding the structure of drives and directories, see Chapter 6 before following the instructions below.

Opening a File from Another Drive or Directory

1) Click **File**, click **Open**.

2) If the presentation is on another drive then click the drop down arrow to the right of the **Drives** box, click on the drive you need. Examine the list of files underneath the **File name** box.

   If you can see your presentation at this point click on it, then click **OK**.

3) To see the contents of a directory, double click on it in the **Directories** box. Examine the files underneath **File name** box. Once you have found your File click on it and click **OK**.

4) A single directory may contain other directories. Double click on these to see what is contained in them.

Bulleted List - I

Creating a Simple Bulleted List

1) Click the **New Page** button at | New Page... | the bottom of the screen.

2) Select **Bulleted List**.

3) Click **Click here to type bulleted list**.

4) Start to type your list. Whenever you press **<Enter>** on the keyboard to start a new line a new bullet will appear.

Figure 7.3 - A bulletted list.

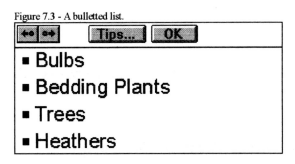

- Bulbs
- Bedding Plants
- Trees
- Heathers

5) If you wish to have a blank line without a bullet, hold down the **<Ctrl>** key on the keyboard and press **<Enter>**.

Figure 7.4 - A bulleted list with blank lines.

- Bulbs

- Bedding Plants

Bulleted List - II

Indenting Text

1) Press **<Enter>** on the keyboard to bring up the next blank line.

2) Remain on the blank line and click this button.

3) Whenever you press **<Enter>** on the keyboard, the cursor will return to the position of the indent.

Figure 7.5 - Indented text.

- **Bulbs**
  - **Daffodil**
  - **Crocus**
  - **Snowdrop**

Decreasing the Indent

1) Press **<Enter>** to bring up a blank indented line.

2) Remain on the blank line and click the following button.

Figure 7.6 - Decreasing the indent.

- **Bulbs**
  - **Daffodil**
  - **Crocus**
  - **Snowdrop**
- **Bedding Plants**

Charts - I

Creating a Bar Chart

1) Click the **New Page** button   New Page...   at the bottom of the screen.

2) Select **1 Chart**.

3) Click **Click here to Create Chart**.

4) Click **Bar** or **3D Bar**.

5) A grid will appear. Type some headings in the legend section - and at least one row of figures starting from row one.

Figure 7.7 - The data sheet for a chart.

	Axis Labels	A	B	C	D
Legend		North	South	East	West
➡					
1		532	678	346	357
2					
3					

6) Click **Edit Titles.**

7) Type a heading for your chart in the **Headings** section. For example, INCOME.

8) Click in the **Axis Titles** section and type some titles for the **X** axis. For example, AREAS.

Type a title for the Y axis. For example POUNDS STERLING.

Click **OK.** You will now see a chart on the screen.

Charts - II

An Example of a Bar Chart

Figure 7.8 - A 3D bar chart.

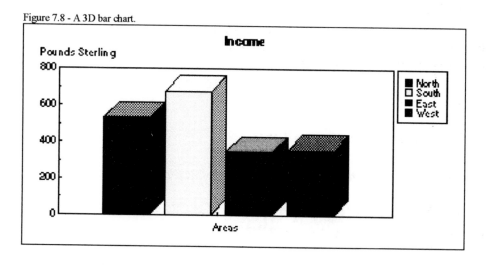

Altering the chart

1) Hover the mouse over the chart and click the *right-hand* mouse button.

2) Click **Edit data and titles**.

3) You are now back at the *Chart Data and Titles screen*.

4) Make your changes.

5) If you wish to alter the *Type* of the chart then click the following button:

6) When you have finished making your alterations, click **OK**.

Tables - I

Creating a Table

1) Click the **New Page** button ⬚ New Page... ⬚ at the bottom of the screen.

2) Select **Table**.

3) Click **Click Here to Create Table**.

4) Choose the number of rows and columns you require.

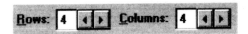

5) Select a style from the options entitled **Choose a Table Style**.

6) Each button depicts the type of lines that will appear around the table.

7) When you have selected both the dimensions and style, click **OK**.

Using the Grid

1) A grid will now appear that you can type into.

2) To get from one box to another, press the **<TAB>** key on the keyboard. Alternatively, click the mouse in the box that you wish to go to.

3) To change the width of the columns, move the mouse onto the vertical lines. The mouse pointer will become a double-headed arrow. Once it has become a double-headed arrow, click the mouse button down and drag it either to the left or to the right.

Tables - II

Changing the Appearance of the Cells

1)   Select the cells you wish to change with the mouse.

2)   Click **Style**.

3)   Click **Attributes[Table]**.

Change the face, size and colour of the text by selecting your
requirements from the drop down boxes.

Figure 7.9 - The face, size and colour option boxes.

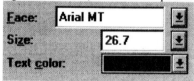

4)   Change the alignment of your cells by selecting them with the mouse
and clicking on the alignment buttons shown below:

Figure 7.10 - Alignment buttons.

Click this button   Click this button   Click this button   Click this button
to left align the   to centre the text   to right align the   to justify the text
text in the cells.   in the cells.   text in the cells.   in the cells.

Tables - III

Changing the Borders and Shading

1) Select either the whole table, or part of the table with the mouse.

2) Click **Style**.

3) Click **Attributes[Table]**.

4) Click **Table background and Border**.

   Change the style of the border by clicking on the arrows to the right of the option boxes.

   Figure 7.11 - Option boxes to change the borders.

   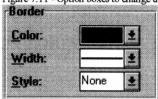

5) Change the background colours and patterns by clicking on the arrows to the right of the option boxes.

   Figure 7. 12 - Option boxes to change the background.

   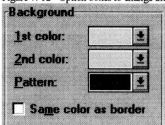

Organisation Charts

Creating an Organisation Chart

1) Click the **New Page** button   `New Page...`
   at the bottom of the screen.

2) Click **Organization Chart**.

3) Click the mouse where it says
   Click here to create Organisation Chart.

4) Select a style from the **Choose A Style** selections.

5) You are then asked to **Type all the entries you want in your chart**.

6) Type a list similar to the one shown below. The most senior individual needs to have his or her name nearest to the left hand margins.

   The subordinates are indented to various levels depending on their positions. To indent a subordinate, press the **<Tab>** key on the keyboard. To create a senior position, press **<Shift>** and **<Tab>**.

Figure 7.13 - List for an organisation chart.

```
Eric Brown
Managing Director
    Enter comment here
  • Jo Smith
    Finance Director
        Enter comment here
      ▪ Sam Fisher
        Accountant
            Enter comment here
      ▪ Sally Fletcher
        Accountant
            Enter comment here
  • Harry Jones
    Production Manager
        Enter comment here
      ▪ Mary Harris
```

7) When you have finished, click **OK** - you will get a chart similar to the one shown below.

Figure 7.14 - An organisation chart.

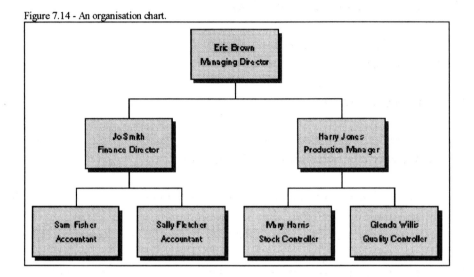

Altering the Chart

1) To alter the chart, double click on it.

2) Click **Edit Text**.

3) Make your changes.

4) Click **OK**.

Screen Shows

Running a Basic Screen Show

1) Click **View**.
   Click **Screen Show**.

2) Click **Run**.

3) Your slides will be displayed on the screen. Press **<Enter>** to take you
   to each one.

Running the Slides Automatically

1) Click **View**.
   Click **Screen Show**.

2) Click **Edit Effects**.
   The *Effects* alter the way in which the slide moves onto the screen.
   Choose an effect.

3) Click **Apply effect to all pages**.

4) Click **Automatically**.

5) Change the **Display Page For** box to the number of seconds you want
   each slide to be displayed for.

6) Click **Apply time to all pages**.

7) Click **Run Show**.

Printing

Printing a Presentation

1) Click **File**.
2) Click **Print**.
3) Click **Print**.

Using the Icon

1) Click this icon.

2) The print menu will appear.

Printing Part of the Presentation

1) Click **File**.
2) Click **Print**.
3) Enter the first page to be printed in the **From Page** box.
4) Enter the last page to be printed in the **to** box.
5) Click **Print**.

Printing Several Copies

1) Click **File**.
2) Click **Print**.
3) Enter the number of copies required in the **Number of copies** box.
4) Click **Print**.

Chapter Eight

Lotus® 123® for Windows®

This chapter was written for Release 5, however in the main the instructions are compatible with the 97 Edition.

Introduction

What is Lotus 123?

Lotus 123 is a spreadsheet package. It is used for storing numerical information. It can be used for recording sales figures, accounting, petty cash or any task which involves calculations.

Screen Layout

The *Menu Bar* appears at the top of the screen.

In addition to the menu bar there are various *Smart Icons* on the screen.

Rows, Columns and Cells

A spreadsheet in Lotus is made up of *Rows* and *Columns*. Each Column is referenced by a letter. Each Row is referenced by a number.

Each *Cell* has a unique cell reference depending on which column and which row it is in. For example if the cursor is in Column A, Row 3 then it is in cell A3.

Figure 8.1 - Cells.

Cell A3

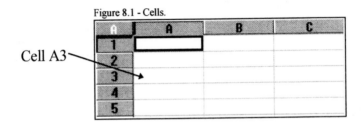

Moving from Cell to Cell

Either:
1)   Use the arrow keys on the keyboard <←> < →> <↑> <↓>, or
2)   Click the mouse in the cell that you wish to move to.

Entering Information into a Cell

1)   Type the information into the appropriate cell.
2)   Either move out of the cell in order for the information to be recorded, or press
     the <**Enter**> key.

The Formula Bar

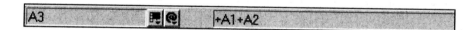

When you type information into the spreadsheet, it appears in the current cell and
also in the formula bar. To alter the information in a cell, click on the cell
concerned and then click on the characters in the formula bar to make your changes.

Sheets

You can use several different sheets within each Lotus file. As a default each file
comes with one sheet. This has a tag which is labelled 'A'. To bring up new sheets
click on **New Sheet**.

Renaming a Sheet

To re-name a sheet tag, double click on the tag and then type in a name.

Saving Spreadsheets

Saving and Naming a Spreadsheet

The first time that you save a spreadsheet you need to give it a name.

1)   Click **File**.
2)   Click **Save As**.
3)   Type a Name for the spreadsheet in **File name**.
4)   Click **OK**.

Saving the Changes to a Spreadsheet

Once you have saved the spreadsheet for the first time and named it, you may need to make changes to it and re-save it. Use the following method for this.

1)   Click **File**.
2)   Click **Save**.

Using the Buttons

Click this button instead of **Save** or **Save As**.

The first time that you click the *save* button in each spreadsheet, the *Save As* screen will appear so that you can name it. When you click this button after the worksheet has been named, the changes will be saved.

Opening Spreadsheets

Opening a File

1) Click **File**.
   Click **Open**.

2) Look in the **File name** box for the file that you are trying to open, and click on it. (If it is not in there, you may need to refer to the section on Opening a File from Another Directory or Folder which follows.)

3) Click **OK**.

Drives and Directories

For help in understanding the structure of drives and directories, see Chapter 6 before following the instructions below.

Opening a File from Another Drive or Directory

1) Click **File**, click **Open**.

2) If the spreadsheet is on another drive then click the drop down arrow to the right of the **Drives** box and click on the drive you need. Examine the contents in the **File name** box.

   If you can see your spreadsheet at this point click on it, then click **OK**.

3) To see the contents of a directory, double click on it in the **Directories** box. Examine the contents in the **File name** box. Once you have found your file click on it and click **Open**.

4) A single directory may contain other directories. Double click on these to see what is contained in them.

Formulas

Entering a Formula

The primary purpose of the spreadsheet is to perform calculations. Each one of these calculations is known as a formula.

1) Go to the cell where you wish the formula to appear.
2) Type in the formula (see simple formulas below).
3) Press the <**Enter**> Key and the answer will appear in the cell.

Simple Formulas

Adding

+A1+A2   This will add the amount in cell A2 to the amount in cell A1.

Subtracting

+A1-A2   This will subtract the amount in A2 from the amount in A1.

Multiplying

+A1*A2   This will multiply the amount in A1 by the amount in A2.

Dividing

+A1/A2   This will divide the amount in A1 by the amount in A2.

Figure 8.2 - Entering formulas.

	A	B	C	D	E
1	2	5	5	8	
2	4	2	2	2	
3	+A1+A2	+B1-B2	+C1*B2	+D1/D2	

Totalling Columns

Using the Keyboard

1) Type a column of figures.

2) Go to the cell in which the total is to appear (in our example A6).
Type the following formula:
@SUM(A1..A5)

A1 and A5 are the first and last cells of the range in the example.

Figure 8.3 - Column of figures.

	A	B	C
1	44		
2	334		
3	523		
4	745		
5	26		
6	@SUM(A1..A5)		

3) Press <**Enter**> and the total will appear.

6	1672		

Using the Autosum Button

1) Type a column of numbers. Select the cells to be added, plus one blank cell for the total (in our example A1 to A6).

2) Click the Sum button to total the column.

	A	B	C
1	44		
2	334		
3	523		
4	745		
5	26		
6	1672 ←		Total

Copying Formulas

Copy Formulas Across Columns

Once you have performed a calculation in the first column of a set of numbers, you can copy the formula to each subsequent column.

1) Perform your calculation for the first column (in our example a total).

Figure 8.4 - Preparing to copy a formula.

	A	B	C	D
1	4	4	3	4
2	3	7	3	6
3	5	2	6	7
4	7	4	4	5
5	2	6	2	3
6	21			

Total

2) Click and drag the mouse over the total and the subsequent cells to the right.

Figure 8.5 - Copying a formula.

	A	B	C	D
1	4	4	3	4
2	3	7	3	6
3	5	2	6	7
4	7	4	4	5
5	2	6	2	3
6	21			

Select these cells

3) Click **Edit**, click **Copy Right**.

Copying Formulas Across Rows

1) Total your first row.

2) Click and drag the mouse over the total and the subsequent cells below.

3) Click **Edit**, click **Copy Down**.

Inserting and Deleting Rows and Columns

Inserting Rows

1) Click in the row underneath where you want the new one to appear.
2) Click **Edit**.
3) Click **Insert**.
4) Select **Row** and click **OK**.

Deleting Rows

1) Click in the row that you wish to delete.
2) Click **Edit**.
3) Click **Delete**.
4) Select **Row** and click **OK**

Inserting Columns

1) Click to the right of where you want the new column to appear.
2) Click **Edit**.
3) Click **Insert**.
4) Select **Column** and click **OK**.

Deleting Columns

1) Click in the column that you wish to delete.
2) Click **Edit**.
3) Click **Delete**.
4) Select **Column** and click **OK**.

Copying and Moving Information

Copying Information

1) Select the cells to be copied with the mouse.
2) Click **Edit**, click **Copy**.
3) Click the mouse at the point where the copy must appear.
4) Click **Edit**, click **Paste**.

Moving Information

1) Select the cells to be moved with the mouse.
2) Click **Edit**, click **Cut**.
3) Click the cursor at the point where the information must reappear.
4) Click **Edit**, click **Paste**.

Using the Icons

1) Select the cells to be moved or copied with the mouse.

Click this button
instead of **Edit**
and **Cut**.

Use this button
instead of **Edit**
and **Copy**.

2) Click at the point where you want the information to appear.

Click this button
instead of **Edit**
and **Paste**.

Deleting

1) Drag the mouse over the cells to be emptied.
2) Click **Edit,** click **Cut,** or press the <**Delete**> key on the keyboard.

For details on how to copy information to another file, see Chapter 4.

Printing

Printing a Sheet

1) Go to the sheet that you wish to print out.
2) Click **File**.
3) Click **Print**.
4) Click **Current Worksheet**.
5) Click **OK**.

Using the Icon

1) Click this icon.

2) This will take you directly to the print menu.

Printing a Selection

1) Select cells to be printed with the mouse.
2) Click **File**.
3) Click **Print**.
4) Click **Selected Range**.
5) Click **OK**.

Printing the Whole File

1) Click **File**.
2) Click **Print**.
3) Click **All Worksheets**.
4) Click **OK**.

Fonts

Changing the Font Size

1) Select the cells to be altered.
2) Click **Style**, click **Font and Attributes**.
3) Select a size from the **Size** box, click **OK**.

Changing the Font Style

1) Select the cells to be altered.
2) Click **Style**, click **Font and Attributes**.
3) Select a typeface from the **Face** box, click **OK**.

Using the buttons

1) Select the text to be altered.
2) Locate the following buttons at the bottom of the screen.

Use this button to   Use this button to
select a font: select a font size:

Bold, Italics and Underline

1) Select the cells to be altered on the mouse.
2) Select one or more of the following buttons:

Use for Bold   Use for Italic   Use for Underline

3) To take one of the enhancements off, select the area to be altered and click the button again. Occasionally you may have to click the same button twice if you have selected a mixed area.

Alignment of Cells

Changing the Alignment

Information can be lined up in the cell in three different ways:

Figure 8.6 - Alignment of cells.

On the left	In the middle	On the right
Item One	9876	986
Item Two	98	98
Item Three	0987	987

1) Select the cells to be altered with the mouse.

2) Click this button to left   Click this button to   Click this button to
    align cells: centre the cells: right align the cells:

The Default

Unless you change the alignment of your cells, numbers will always align on the right hand side of the cells, and text will always align on the left hand side.

Figure 8.7 - Default alignment.

Site	Employees
Town Centre	23
Industrial Estate	124
Business Centre	34

Charts - I

Creating a Bar Chart

1) Type the categories and the relevant figures into a group of cells, placing the categories above the figures.

Figure 8.8 - Figures prepared for a chart.

London	Crawley	Hove	Brighton
600	500	200	300

2) Select all of the information with the mouse.

3) Click the Chart icon.

4) Single click in the middle of the spreadsheet.

5) A graph will appear on the screen. To resize it, move the mouse onto the dots around the edge, click and drag to the required size.

Figure 8.9 - A bar chart in Lotus.

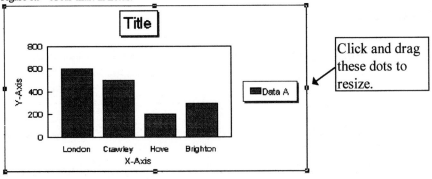

Charts - II

Changing the Chart Type

1) Make sure that your graph is selected. If it is not then single click on the middle of it.

2) Click **Chart,** click **Type.**

    Alternatively click
    this button.

3) Select the type that you want from the **Types** list, click **OK.**

Inserting Headings for the X and Y Axis

1) Make sure that your graph is selected. If it is not then single click on the middle of it.

2) Click **Chart,** click **Axis.**

3) Click **Y-Axis,** type in an **Axis Title,** click **OK.**
    Repeat this step for the X-Axis.

Inserting a Title

1) Double click on the *Title* label that is
    already on the graph.

2) Type a name for the chart in **Line 1,** click **OK.**

Chapter Nine

My Computer®

This chapter was written for Windows 95®. However in the main the instructions are compatible with Windows 98®.

Getting Started

What is My Computer?

My Computer is a utility for organising the information on your computer. There are facilities for creating directories, copying files, moving files and deleting files.

Launching My Computer

1) Locate the My Computer icon. It is situated on the *Desktop*. The Desktop is the screen that you see when you first turn on your computer.

Figure 9.1 - *My Computer* icon.

2) Double click the **My Computer** icon.

Screen Layout

Once you have launched *My Computer* you will see a window that contains a *Menu Bar* and a set of icons representing various drives.

Figure 9.2 - *My Computer* window.

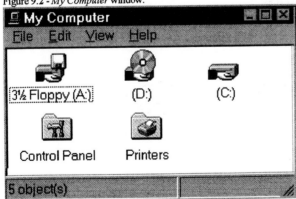

The Drives

What are Drives?

Drives are the physical storage devices that your computer uses to store data. Once you have launched My Computer you will see a number of icons depicting various drives. These may vary slightly depending on the configuration of your machine.

To view the contents of a drive, double click on the relevant icon.

The Most Common Drives

1) **The [C:] Drive**

   The [C:] drive is the hard drive located inside your computer. This contains all the files which enable your computer to run.

2) **The [A:] Drive**

   The [A:] Drive is the small drive in front of your computer. This is the one that you put floppy disks into.

3) **The [D:] Drive**

   This is usually the CD-ROM drive.

Folders

What are Folders?

The information on your drives needs to be organised. Folders are used to house files. Each folder is given a name that is relevant to the files that are contained within it.

To view the folders on your C drive, launch **My Computer** and then double click on the **[C:]** icon. You will now see a number of folders.

Figure 9.3 - A folder.

Viewing the Contents of a Folder

Figure 9.4 - A window showing the contents of a folder.

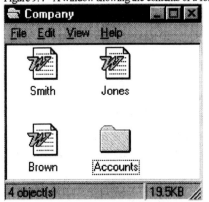

To view the contents of a folder, double click on it and a window will appear containing all of the information held in it.

To close it again, click the *Close* **X** in the top right hand corner of the window.

Sub-directories

Another term used to describe a folder is 'directory'. A sub-directory is therefore a folder within a folder. If you look at the contents of the Company folder shown above, you will see that it contains another folder called 'accounts'.

Creating Folders

Choose a Position for the New Folder

Firstly you need to decide where you would like your new folder to be placed.

If you want it to be directly on the **[C:]** drive, then launch **My Computer** and double click on the **[C:]** icon.

If you want to position it *inside* an existing folder, then you need to locate this folder, and double click on it to open it up.

Creating the Folder

At this point there may be several different windows open all over your screen, each with its own menu bar.

Use the menu bar that runs across the top of the window which will eventually house your new folder.

1) Click **File**.

2) Select **New**.

3) Select **Folder**.

4) A new folder will now appear on your screen containing the words 'New Folder'. Click the mouse on the words 'New Folder' on this icon and rename it to suit you.

Figure 9.5 - Renaming new folders.

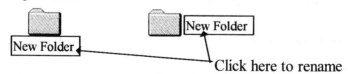

5) Press **<Enter>**.

Copying Files

Copying Documents to a Floppy Disk

1) Double click on the **My Computer** icon, double click the **[C:]** icon.

2) Double click the folder that contains the document/s to be copied.

3) Single click the document to be copied. (To select more than one file, press the <Ctrl> key on the keyboard and single click the additional files required.)

4) Click **Edit**, click **Copy**.

5) Close down the folders that you have opened, using the *Close* **X** .

6) Ensure that you have a floppy disk in the drive. Double click on the **[A:]** icon.

7) Click **Edit** , click **Paste**.

Copying Documents to Another Folder

1) Double click on the **My Computer** icon, double click the **[C:]** icon.

2) Double click the folder that contains the document/s to be copied.

3) Single click the document to be copied. (To select more than one file, press the <Ctrl> key on the keyboard and single click the additional files required.)

4) Click **Edit**, click **Cut**.

5) Close down the folders that you have opened.

6) Double click on the folder that you wish to copy the document to.

7) Click **Edit,** click **Paste**.

Moving Files

Moving Documents to a Floppy Disk

1)   Double click on the **My Computer** icon, double click the **[C:]** icon.

2)   Double click the folder that contains the document/s to be copied.

3)   Single click the document to be copied. (To select more than one file, press the **<Ctrl>** key on the keyboard and single click the additional files required.)

4)   Click **Edit**, click **Cut**.

5)   Close down the folders that you have opened.

6)   Ensure that you have a floppy disk in the drive. Double click on the **[A:]** icon.

7)   Click **Edit** , click **Paste**.

Moving Documents to Another Folder

1)   Double click on the **My Computer** icon, double click the **[C:]** icon.

2)   Double click the folder that contains the document/s to be copied.

3)   Single click the document to be copied. (To select more than one file, press the **<Ctrl>** key on the keyboard and single click the additional files required.)

4)   Click **Edit**, click **Copy**.

5)   Close down the folders that you have opened.

6)   Double click on the folder that you wish to copy the document to.

7)   Click **Edit,** click **Paste**.

Deleting Files and Folders

Deleting Files or Folders

Single click the mouse on the file or folder that you wish to delete. Press the **<Delete>** key on the keyboard.

Deleting Several Files at Once

Alternatively, put your hand on the **<Ctrl>** key of the keyboard and click on several files. Press the **<Delete>** key on the keyboard.

Chapter Ten

Corel® Paradox® for Windows®

This section was written for version 8.

Getting Started

Corel Paradox is used for creating databases. Databases are used to record information such as the details of all your customers or suppliers. The information can be interrogated in order to find records that meet set criteria.

Screen Layout

The *Menu Bar* appears at the top of the screen.

In addition to the menu bar there are various *buttons*.

The Project Viewer Menu appears down the left hand side of the screen.

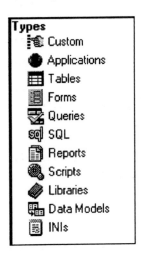

Tables

What are Tables?

A table is a grid of information. Each box in the grid is known as a field. A row of fields is known as a record.

Figure 10.1 - A table.

Company	Town	County
Longleys Glass	Crawley	Sussex
Browns Repairs	Hove	Sussex
Shorts Shoes	Brighton	Sussex

Creating a Table

1)   Click **File**, click **New**.

2)   Make sure that Corel Paradox is showing in the box at the top. If it is not then click the drop down arrow and select it.

3)   Click **[New Table]**, click **Create**, click **Blank**.
      Make sure the table type is **Paradox**, click **OK**.

4)   Type in a **Field Name**: for example, COMPANY.

      Click in **Type**, click the *right-hand* mouse button, click **Alpha**. If it is to contain numbers only, then choose **Number**.

      Click in **Size**. Stipulate the maximum amount of characters that can be held in the field. For example, 20. (This is not required for a number field.)

5)   Repeat step 4 for each field you require.

Figure 10.2 - Creating field headings.

Field Name	Type	Size	Key
Customer	A	20	
Town	A	20	

6)   On completion click **File,** click **Save As**. Give the table a name. Click **Save**.

Using the Table

Opening the Table

To open a table that you have created:

1) Click **File**.
2) Click **Open**.
3) Click **Table**.
4) Select your table, click **Open**.

Figure 10.3 - An empty table.

Rec	Company	Town	County

Entering Information

1) Click the *Edit Data* icon.

2) A empty row will appear in order for you to enter information.

Figure 10.4 - A table with a blank row.

Rec	Company	Town	County

3) Use the <**Tab**> key on the keyboard to take you to the next box. Use <**Shift**>and<**Tab**> to go back. A new row will appear on the table when you have made at least one entry and pressed the <**Tab**> key in the last box.

4) When you have finished entering information, click **File**, click **Close**.

Finding Information

1) Go to the column that contains the data that you are looking for.

2) Click **Record**, click **Locate**, click **Value**.

3) Enter the item you are looking for in **Value**, click **OK**.

Key Fields

What is a Key Field?

It is customary to give each record a unique number. This is known as a *Key Field*.

Figure 10..5 - A table structure with a key field.

Rec	Company	Town	County
1	Longleys Glass	Crawley	Sussex
2	Browns Repairs	Hove	Sussex
3	Shorts Shoes	Brighton	Sussex

← Key Field

Creating a Table with a Key Field

1) Click **File**, click **New**.

2) Make sure that Corel Paradox is showing in the box at the top. If it is not, then click the drop down arrow and select it.

3) Click **[New Table]**, click **Create**, click **Blank**.
   Make sure the table type says **Paradox**, click **OK**.

4) Click in **Field Name** - and type a name for your key field.
   For example, REC.

5) Click in **Type**. Click the right-hand mouse button, click **+Autoincrement**.

6) Click in **Key** and press any letter to put a star in the box.

7) Now create the rest of the fields that you require in the normal way, then save and close.

Changing the Structure of a Table

Restructuring the Table

Occasionally you will need to add new fields to your table, or delete existing ones.

1) Click **File** and **Open**.

2) Click **Table**.

3) Hold the mouse over the table to be altered, click the right hand mouse button and select **Restructure**.

4) Make the changes to the structure of your table.

5) Click **Save**.

Deleting a Field

1) You can delete a field whilst *restructuring* your table.

2) Go to the field that you wish to delete.

3) Hold down the <**Ctrl**> key on the keyboard and press <**Delete**>.

Query Design

What is a Query?

Once you have keyed some information into your table, you may wish to query it to pull out sets of information. For example you might want to pull out all of the customers who are based in Brighton.

Creating a Query

1) Click **File**, click **New**.

2) Make sure that it says Corel Paradox in the box at the top.

3) Click **[New Query]**.

4) Click **Create**.

5) Select the table that you wish to query. Click **Open**.

6) A grid showing the names of the fields in your table will appear on the screen.

7) Each field name has a box underneath it. If you wish to see that field in your query, then put a tick in it.

8) Input the information that you want to search for next to the tick box. The following example shows a query that will select all of the companies in Brighton on your database.

Figure 10.6 - A query to show all the companies in Brighton.

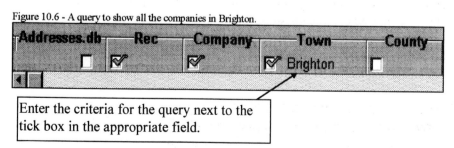

Enter the criteria for the query next to the tick box in the appropriate field.

9) To view the completed query, click **Query**, click **Run Query**.

Queries on Numbers

Explanation

You way want to create some queries that use mathematical operators. For example, you might want to pick out all customers who have ordered over 200 items.

Use an Appropriate Table

You can only create a query that involves numbers if the *field* that you are querying on has a *Number* data type. Make sure that you select Number from the **Type** box when you are creating your original table.

Figure 10.7 - Design a table with a *number* data type.

Field Name	Type	Size	Key
Customer	A	20	
Town	A	20	
Quantity Ordered	N		

Designing the Query

Design the query in the normal way. Input the information that you want to search for next to the tick box in the appropriate field.

>200   will pull out everybody who has ordered over 200 items.
<200   will pull out everybody who has ordered less than 200 items.
=200   will pull out everybody who has ordered exactly 200 items.

The following example shows a query that will pull out all customers who have ordered over 200 items.

Figure 10.8 - A query to pull out customers that have ordered more than 200 items.

Addresses.DB	Company	Town	Quantity Ordered
☐	☑	☑	☑ >200

Creating a Form

What is a Form?

Instead of entering information directly into the table, you can use a form. Only one record is displayed at a time, making it easier to use.

Figure 10.9 - A table and a form.

Rec	Company	Town	County
1	Longleys Glass	Crawley	Sussex
2	Browns Repairs	Hove	Sussex
3	Shorts Shoes	Brighton	Sussex

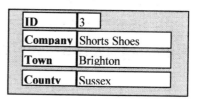

Creating a Form

1) Ensure that you have already created a table with the relevant fields.

2) Click **File**, click **New**.

3) Make sure that **Corel Paradox** is showing in the box at the top.

4) Click **[New Forms]**.

5) Click **Create**.

6) Click **Data Model**.

7) Select the table that you wish to base your form on. Click **OK**.

8) Choose a **Layout**. Click **OK**.

9) The structure of the new form is now displayed.

10) Click **File**, click **Close**, click **Yes** to save the changes, provide a **File name**. Click **Save**.

Entering Information into a Form

Opening the Form

1)   Click **File**, click **Open**.

2)   Click **Form**.

3)   Select your form.

4)   Click **Open**.

Inputting Information Using the Data Icon

1)   Open the form.

2)   Click the Edit
      Data icon.

3)   To go to different records you can use these buttons on the toolbar at the top.

4)   Use this button to take you to the next
      record.

5)   Use this button to take you to the previous
      record.

6)   To get to a new blank record, click these
      two buttons in the order shown.

Chapter Eleven

Microsoft® Powerpoint® for Windows®

This section was written for version 97, however in the main the instructions are compatible with versions 4 and 7.

Getting Started

What is Powerpoint?

Powerpoint is used for creating presentations. These presentations can be in the form of acetates for an overhead projector; alternatively, the slides can be shown directly onto a computer screen.

Creating a New Presentation

1) Launch Powerpoint.
At the *New Presentation* menu, ensure that **Blank Presentation** is selected. Click **OK.**

2) If Powerpoint is already running:
click **File**, click **New**,
select the **Blank Presentation Template**, click **OK.**

3) You will now see a number of layouts.

Choose the *Title* slide.

4) Click **OK**.

Using the Slide

1) Click on the words **Click Here to Add Title**.

Click here to add title

2) Type your text, e.g. BUSINESS PLAN.

3) Click outside of the place-holder when you have finished.

BUSINESS PLAN

4) Repeat the process for the subtitle.

Working with Several Slides

Creating Another Slide

1) Create your presentation and first slide in the normal way.

2) Locate the *Common Task Toolbar* on the screen. If it is not displayed, then click **View**, click **Toolbars**, click **Common Tasks**.

Figure 11.1 - The *Common Task* toolbar.

Click **New Slide**.

3) Choose another layout, click **OK**.

Slide Sorter

1) Click on the *Slide Sorter* button. This is located on the bottom left hand corner of the screen.

2) All of your slides will now be displayed on the screen in miniature.

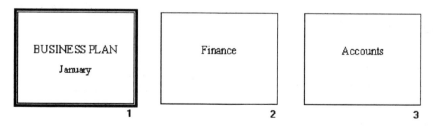

3) Double click on the slide that you want to look at in greater detail.

4) You can also use the *Slide Sorter* to click and drag the slides to different positions.

Saving Presentations

Saving and Naming a Presentation

The first time that you save a presentation you need to give it a name.

1) Click **File**.
2) Click **Save As**.
3) Type a name for the presentation in **File name**.
4) Click **Save**.

Saving the Changes to a Presentation

Once you have saved the presentation for the first time and named it, you may need to make changes to it and re-save it. Use the following method for this.

1) Click **File**.
2) Click **Save**.

Using the Buttons

Click this button instead of **Save** or **Save As**.

The first time that you click the *Save* button in each presentation, the *Save As* screen will appear so that you can name it. When you click this button after the worksheet has been named, the changes will be saved.

Opening Presentations

Opening a Presentation

1) Click **File**.
    Click **Open**.

2) Look in the list of files to find the presentation that you are trying to open, and then click on it. (If it is not in there, you may need to refer to the section below on 'Opening a Presentation from Another Drive or Folder'.)

3) Click **Open**.

Drives and Folders

For help in understanding the structure of drives and folders, see Chapters 5 and 9 before following the instructions below.

Opening a Presentation from Another Drive or Folder

1) Click **File**, click **Open**.

2) If the presentation is on another drive then click the drop down arrow to the right of the **Look in** box, and double click on the drive you need.

    If you can see your presentation at this point click on it, then click **Open**.

3) To see the contents of a folder, double click on it in the **Look in** box. A single folder may contain other folders, so double click on these to view their contents.

4) Once you have found your presentation click on it.

5) Click **Open**.

Bulleted Lists - I

Creating a Bulleted List

1) Click **New Slide** on the Common Task Toolbar.

2) Select the *Bulleted List* Layout.

3) Click the mouse on the words **Click to Add Text**.

   • Click to add text

4) Type in your information and press **<Enter>** on the keyboard. As you press **<Enter>** another bullet will appear.

5) When you have finished, click outside of the place-holder.

   • Monday
   • Tuesday
   • Wednesday
   • Thursday
   • Friday

   Click here when you have finished

Putting Blank Lines Between the Bullets

1) Create your bulleted list in the normal way.

2) Type the information for the first line (do not press **<Enter>**).

3) Hold down the **<Shift>** key and press **<Enter>**. Now press **<Enter>** on its own to get your next bullet.

4) You should now have a space between your lines.

   • Monday

   • Tuesday

Bulleted Lists - II

Promoting and Demoting Indents

You may wish to *promote* or *demote* the indentation of your bulleted list.

Figure 11.2 - Bulleted lists - promoted and demoted.

Begin on the left ────────────────→
Text promoted to next setting ─────→

Text demoted back ──────────────→
Text promoted again ──────────────→

| • **Monday** |
| - Arrive at 9.00am |
| - Set up stand |
| - Depart at 3.00pm |
| • **Tuesday** |
| - Arrive at 10.00am |
| - Show begins at 11.00am |
| - Depart at 5.00pm |

1) Type the first line.
   Press the **<Enter>** key on the keyboard to get another bullet.

   • **Monday**
   •

2) Click the *Promote* button on the toolbar.

3) The bullet will now be promoted.

   • **Departments**
   -

4) Type the indented lines of information.

   • **Departments**
   - Finance
   - Marketing

5) Press **<Enter>** again and get another indented line.

   • **Departments**
   - Finance
   - Marketing
   -

6) Press the *Demote* button to change the current line to a normal bullet.

Organisation Charts - I

What is an Organisation Chart?

Organisation charts are often used to show the structure of a company.

Figure 11.3 - An organisation chart.

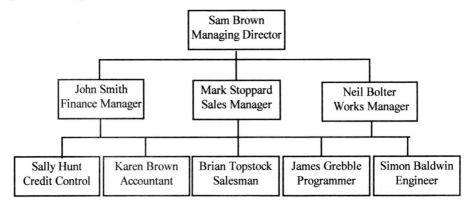

Starting an Organisation Chart

1) Click **New Slide** on the Common Task Toolbar.

2) Select the *Organisation Chart* Layout.

3) Double click on the *Organisation Chart* icon in the middle of the slide.

Organisation Charts - II

Creating the Chart

1) Once you have launched the organisation chart, you will see the structure of an organisation chart.

Figure 11.4 - Structure for an organisation chart.

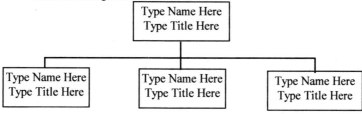

2) Click the mouse on the box at the top of the structure and type a name, press <**Enter**> and type a title. Repeat this step in order to type in the three boxes on the line below.

Adding a Subordinate

1) Click the Subordinate Button.

2) Click the box showing the name of the person that the subordinate reports to.

Figure 11.5 - Adding a subordinate.

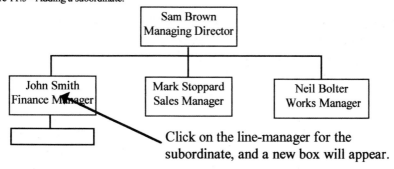

Click on the line-manager for the subordinate, and a new box will appear.

Organisation Charts - III

Adding a Co-Worker

1) Click one of the co-worker buttons.

2) Click the box that contains the name of the co-worker's colleague.

Figure 11.6 - Adding a co-worker.

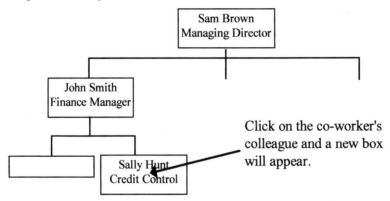

Click on the co-worker's colleague and a new box will appear.

Adding a Manager

1) Click the Manager button.

2) Click the box containing the name of the person that the new manager is responsible for.

Figure 11.7 - Adding a manager.

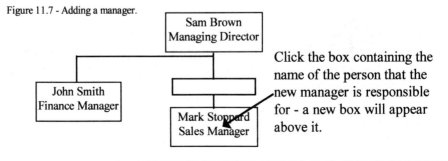

Click the box containing the name of the person that the new manager is responsible for - a new box will appear above it.

Organisation Charts - IV

Adding an Assistant

1) Click the Assistant button.

2) Click the box containing the name of the person who is to have an assistant.

Figure 11.8 - Adding an assistant.

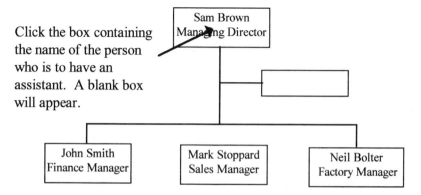

Click the box containing the name of the person who is to have an assistant. A blank box will appear.

Deleting a Box

1) Click on the edge of the box to delete.

2) Press the <**Delete**> key on the keyboard.

Saving your Organisation Chart

1) Click **File**. (From the organisation chart menu, not the powerpoint menu.) If you accidentally click behind the Powerpoint window then the chart will become a large shaded box within your presentation. To get back to the chart, click on the large shaded box.

2) Click **Update Presentation**. Click **File**, click **Close and return to presentation**.

Organisation Charts - V

Changing the Colour of the Boxes

1) Click **Edit**.
   Click **Select**, click **All**.

2) Click **Boxes**.
   Click **Color**.
   Select a colour.

Changing the Thickness of the Lines

1) Click **Edit**.
   Click **Select**, click **All**.

2) Click **Lines**.
   Click **Thickness**.
   Select a different thickness.

Changing the Line Colour

1) Click **Edit**.
   Click **Select**, click **All**.

2) Click **Lines**.
   Click **Color**.
   Select a different colour.

Organisation Charts - VI

Changing the Fonts

1) Click **Edit**.
   Click **Select**, click **All**.

2) Click **Text**, click **Font**.

3) Select a font from the **Font** box.
   Select a font style (such as Bold, Italic or Underline) from the **Font Style** box.
   Select a font size from the **Size** box.

4) Click **OK**.

Changing the Justification of the Text

1) Click **Edit**.
   Click **Select**, click **All**.

2) Click **Text**.

3) Click right to make the text go to the right of the boxes.

```
                        Sam Brown
                  Managing Director
```

Click centre to make the text go the centre of the boxes.

```
                  Sam Brown
                Managing Director
```

Click left to make the text go to the left of the boxes.

```
Sam Brown
Managing Director
```

Charts

Creating a Chart

1) Click **New Slide** on the Common Task Toolbar.

2) Select the *Chart* Layout.

3) Double click on the chart icon in the middle of the screen.

4) A data sheet will appear on the screen showing some pre-typed information.

		A	B	C	D
		1st Qtr	2nd Qtr	3rd Qtr	4th Qtr
1	East	20.4	27.4	90	20.4
2	West	30.6	38.6	34.6	31.6
3	North	45.9	46.9	45	43.9

Presentation - Datasheet

5) Delete all of the information from the data sheet.

6) Type in the information for your chart.

Figure 11.9 - Preparing the data for the chart.

		A	B	C	D
		Jan	Feb	Mar	April
1	3-D Colum	6	8	3	4
2					

Presentation - Datasheet

7) Click the *Close* **X** on the data sheet.

Slide Shows

Slide Show Button

1) Use the slide sorter button to get to your first slide.

2) Click the slide show button. You will find this
    on the bottom left hand corner of the screen.

3) Your slide will now be blown up to full size on the screen.
    Press the **<Enter>** key on the keyboard to see each slide in turn.

4) Use the **<Esc>** key if you wish to come out of the full screen setting before you
    have finished viewing all your slides.

Setting the Timings and Effects

1) Go to the Slide Sorter view.

2) Click **Edit**, click **Select All**, click **Slide Show**.
    Click **Slide Transition**.

3) In the **Advance** box, click **Automatically After** and the number of seconds
    you require.

4) Click the drop down arrow on the **Effect** box, select an effect such as 'Box In'.
    Click **Apply to All**.

Running the Show

1) Use the slide sorter button to get to your first slide.
    Make sure that you have set your timings and effects.

2) Click **Slide Show**.
    Click **View** Show.

3) Use the *Slide Show* button to view the show again.

Chapter Twelve

Corel® Quattro Pro® for Windows®

This section was written for version 8.

Introduction

What is Quattro Pro?

Quattro Pro is a spreadsheet package. It is used for storing numerical information. It can be used for recording sales figures, accounting, petty cash or any task which involves calculations.

Notebooks

Each file in Quattro Pro is called a *Notebook*.

Screen Layout

The *Menu Bar* appears at the top of the screen.

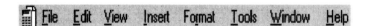

In addition to the menu bar there are various *Buttons* on the screen.

Rows, Columns and Cells

A notebook in Quattro Pro is made up of *Rows* and *Columns*. Each column is referenced by a letter. Each row is referenced by a number.

Each cell has a unique *cell reference* depending on which column and which row it is in. For example, if the cursor is in Column A, Row 3 then it is in cell A3.

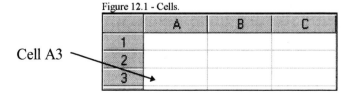

Figure 12.1 - Cells.

Cell A3

Moving from Cell to Cell

Either:
1)   Use the arrow keys on the keyboard <←> < →> <↑> <↓>, or
2)   Press <**Enter**> to go down one cell at a time, or
3)   Click the mouse in the cell that you wish to move to.

Entering Information into a Cell

1)   Type the information into the appropriate cell.
2)   Always move out of the cell in order for the information to be recorded.

The Formula Bar

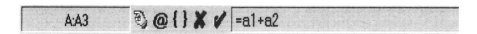

As soon as you start to type a formula into a cell, it will appear in the formula bar.
To alter a formula, click on the cell that contains the formula, click on the formula
bar, make your alteration, then click the blue tick.

What are Sheets?

There are several sheets in each notebook. Each sheet can be used for a different
purpose. For example, one sheet could be used for SALES and another for
EXPENSES. To get to each sheet, single click on the sheet tags at the bottom of
the screen.

Renaming a Sheet

To re-name a sheet tag, double click on the tag.

Saving Notebooks

Saving and Naming a Notebook

The first time that you save a notebook, you need to give it a name.

1) Click **File**.
2) Click **Save As**.
3) Type a name for the notebook in **File Name**.
4) Click **Save**.

Saving the Changes to a Notebook

Once you have saved the notebook for the first time and named it, you may need to make changes to it and re-save it. Use the following method for this.

1) Click **File**.
2) Click **Save**.

Using the Buttons

Click this button instead of **Save** or **Save As**.

The first time that you click the *save* button in each workbook, the *Save As* screen will appear so that you can name it. When you click this button after the worksheet has been named, the changes will be saved.

.

Opening Notebooks

Opening a Notebook

1) Click **File**, click **Open**.

2) Look in the **Look in** box for the file that you are trying to open, and click on it. (If it is not in there then you may need to refer to the section below on 'Opening a Notebook from Another Drive or Folder'.)

3) Click **Open**.

Drives and Folders

For help in understanding the structure of drives and folders, see Chapters 5 and 9 before following the instructions below.

Opening a Notebook from Another Drive or Folder

1) Click **File**, click **Open**.

2) If the notebook is on another drive, then click the drop down arrow to the right of the **Look in** box, and double click on the drive you need.

   If you can see your notebook at this point, click on it, then click **Open**.

3) To see the contents of a folder, double click on it. A single folder may contain other folders: double click on these to view their contents.

4) Once you have found your notebook click on it.

5) Click **Open**.

Formulas

Entering a Formula

The primary purpose of the spreadsheet is to perform calculations. Each one of these calculations is known as a *formula*.

1) Go to the cell where you wish the formula to appear.
2) Type in the formula (see simple formulas below).
3) Press the <**Enter**> key and the answer will appear in the cell.

Simple Formulas

Adding

=A1+A2   This will add the amount in cell A1 to the amount in cell A2.

Subtracting

=A1-A2   This will subtract the amount in cell A2 from the amount in cell A1.

Multiplying

=A1*A2   This will multiply the amount in cell A1 by the amount in cell A2.

Dividing

=A1/A2   This will divide the amount in cell A1 by the amount in cell A2.

Figure 12.2 - Entering formulas.

	A	B	C	D	E
1	2	5	5	8	
2	4	2	2	2	
3	=A1+A2	=B1-B2	=C1*B2	=D1/D2	

Totalling Columns

Using the Keyboard

1) Type a column of figures.

2) Go to the cell in which the total is to appear (in our example, A5).
Type the following formula: **=SUM(A1:A4)**
A1 and A4 are the first and last cells of the range in the example.

Figure 12.3 - Column of figures.

	A	B	C	D
1	4			
2	3			
3	5			
4	2			
5	=SUM(A1:A4)			

3) Press **<Enter>** on the keyboard and the total will appear.

6	=SUM(A1:A4)			

Using the Quicksum Button

1) Select all the cells to be totalled with the mouse, plus one extra cell for the total. In our example we will choose cells A1 to A5.

Figure 12.4 - Select the cells to sum.

	A	B	C	D
1	4			
2	3		Select the column of	
3	5		cells plus one extra	
4	7		cell for the total.	
5				

2) Click the
quicksum
button.

3) Look in the formula bar to check that the range is correct.

Quickfill

Duplicating Formulas Across Columns

Once you have performed a calculation in the first column of a set of numbers, you can copy the formula to each subsequent column using *Quickfill*.

1) Perform your calculation in the first column (in our example, a total).

Figure 12.5 - Preparing to duplicate totals.

	A	B	C	D
1	4	4	3	4
2	3	7	3	6
3	5	2	6	7
4	7	4	4	5
5	19			

Total

2) Click and drag the mouse over the total and the subsequent cells to the right.

Figure 12.6 - Duplicating the totals.

	A	B	C	D
1	4	4	3	4
2	3	7	3	6
3	5	2	6	7
4	7	4	4	5
5	19			

Select these cells

3) Click **Edit**, click **Fill**, click **Quickfill**.

Duplicating Formulas Down Rows

1) Total your first row.

2) Click and drag the mouse over the total and the subsequent cells below.

3) Click **Edit**, click **Fill**, click **Quickfill**.

Copying and Moving Information

Copying Information

1) Highlight the cells to be copied by dragging over them with the mouse.
2) Click **Edit**, click **Copy**.
3) Click the mouse into the cell where the copy must appear.
4) Click **Edit**, click **Paste**.

Moving Information

1) Select the cells to be moved with the mouse.
2) Click **Edit**, click **Cut**.
3) Click the cursor at the point where the information must reappear.
4) Click **Edit**, click **Paste**.

Using the Icons

1) Select the cells to be moved or copied with the mouse.

Use this button instead of **Edit** and **Cut**.   Use this button instead of **Edit** and **Copy**.

2) Click at the point where you want the information to appear.

Use this button instead of **Edit** and **Paste**

Deleting

1) Drag the mouse over the cells to be emptied.
2) Click **Edit,** click **Cut**, or press the **<Delete>** key on the keyboard.

For details on how to copy information to another file, see Chapter 4.

Inserting and Deleting Rows and Columns

Inserting Rows

1) Click in the row underneath where you want the new one to appear.
2) Click **Insert**.
3) Click **Row**.

Deleting Rows

1) Click in the row that you wish to delete.
2) Click **Edit,** click **Delete**.
3) Click in **Dimensions**, select **Rows**.
4) Click **OK**.

Inserting Columns

1) Click to the right of where you want the new column to appear.
2) Click **Insert**.
3) Click **Column**.

Deleting Columns

1) Click in the column that you wish to delete.
2) Click **Edit,** click **Delete**.
3) Click in **Dimensions**, select **Columns**.
4) Click **OK**.

Using the Icons

Click this button instead of **Insert** and **Row**.

Use this icon instead of **Edit** and **Delete**.

Printing

Printing a Sheet

1) Make sure that the sheet you want to print is displayed on the screen.
2) Click **File**, click **Print**.
3) Click **Current Sheet**.
4) Click **Print** (at the bottom of the dialogue box).

Using the Icon

1) Click this icon:

2) This will send one copy of all the pages of your current sheet to print.

Printing a Selection of Cells

1) Select cells to be printed with the mouse.
2) Click **File**.
3) Click **Print**.
4) Click **Selection**.
5) Click **Print**.

Printing the Whole Workbook

1) Click **File**.
2) Click **Print**.
3) Click **Notebook**.
4) Click **Print**.

Format of Cells

Changing the Font Size

1) Select the cells to be altered with the mouse.
2) Click the drop down arrow to the right of the following icon:
   [10 ▼] When the list of sizes drops down, you will see a scroll bar on the right hand side of the list - use this to see other numbers.
3) Select the size you want by clicking on the actual number.

Changing the Font Style

1) Select the cells to be altered with the mouse.
2) Click the drop down arrow to the right of the following icon:
   [Arial ▼] When the list of fonts drops down, you will see a scroll bar on the right hand side of the list - use this to find more fonts.
3) Select the font you want by clicking on its name.

Bold, Italics and Underline

1) Select the cells to be altered on the mouse.
2) Select one or more of the following buttons:

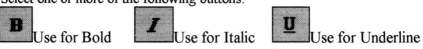 **B** Use for Bold   *I* Use for Italic   U̲ Use for Underline

3) To take one of the enhancements off, select the area to be altered and click the button again. Occasionally you may have to click the same button twice if you have selected a mixed area.

Alignment of Cells

Changing the Alignment of Cells

1)   Select the cells to be changed with the mouse.

2)   Click the Alignment   Select the Alignment
     icon.   option that you want from
                                                   the available choices.

Alignment Options

 The default. Numbers align on the right, text on the left.

Sales	
	876
Expenses	
	987

 This button will align all information on the left.

Sales
876
Expenses
987

 This button will align all information on the right.

Sales	
	876
Expenses	
	987

 This button will align all information in the centre.

Sales
876
Expenses
987

 Select some adjacent cells, click this button, the text will align between them.

Figures	
1995	

 This button will indent the first line of the cell.

Expenses
1998

139

Charts - I

Creating a Pie Chart

1) Type the categories and the figures into a group of cells, placing the categories above the figures.

Figure 12.7 - Figures prepared for a chart.

London	Crawley	Hove	Brighton
600	500	200	300

2) Select all of the information with the mouse.

3) Click **Insert**, click **Chart**, click **Next**.

4) The pie is the default setting, so click **Next** again.

5) Choose a specific type of pie, then click **Next**.

6) Select a colour scheme, then click **Next**.

7) Type a **Title** for the chart, for example: Sales. Click **Finish**.

8) Click anywhere on the spreadsheet and a graph will appear.

Figure 12.8 - A pie chart.

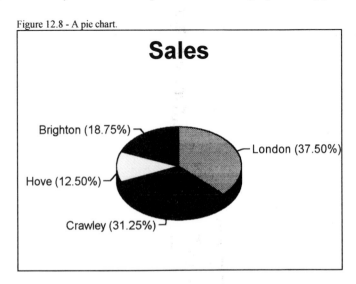

Charts - II

Creating a Bar Chart

1) Type the categories and the relevant figures into a group of cells, placing the categories above the figures.

Figure 12.9 - Figures prepared for a chart.

London	Crawley	Hove	Brighton
600	500	200	300

2) Select all of the information with the mouse.

3) Click **Insert**, click **Chart**, click **Next**.

4) Choose **Bar**, click **Next** again.
Choose a specific type of bar chart, then click **Next**.

5) Select a colour scheme, then click **Next**.

6) Type a **Title** for the chart, for example: Sales.
Type a heading for the X axis, for example: Towns.
Type a heading for the Y axis, for example: Amounts.
Click **Finish**.

7) Click anywhere on the spreadsheet and a graph will appear.

Figure 12.10 - A bar chart.

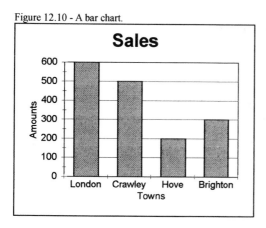

Charts - III

The Chart Button Bar

When a chart that you have created is selected, the chart button bar will be available on the screen. If you cannot see the button bar, then single click on the white area between the chart and the box that surrounds it. The button bar should now come into view.

Changing the Type of Chart

1) Create a chart and ensure that it is still selected. If it is not, then single click it with the mouse.

2) Click on this button from the Chart Button Bar.

3) Select a different chart type.

Changing the Main Title and Titles for X and Y Axis

1) Make sure that the Chart Button Bar is displayed.

2) Click the Titles button.

3) Make your changes Click **OK**.

Chapter Thirteen

Recycle Bin®

This chapter was written for Windows 95®. However in the main the instructions are compatible with Windows 98®.

Getting Started

What is the Recycle Bin?

The Recycle Bin is a utility found on Windows 95 and Windows 98. It is used to store all the documents that you have deleted. If you accidentally delete a document, you can launch the Recycle Bin and *restore* it.

Launching the Recycle Bin

1)   Locate the My Computer icon. It is situated on the *Desktop*. The Desktop is the screen that you see when you first turn on your computer.

Figure 13.1 - The *Recycle Bin* icon.

2)   Double click the **Recycle Bin** icon.

Screen Layout

At the top of the screen there is a *Menu Bar*.

Figure 13.2 - The menu bar.
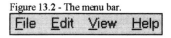

The main part of the screen is taken up with a list of files that have been deleted.

Figure 13.3 - Deleted documents in the Recycle Bin.

Using the Recycle Bin

Restoring a File

1) Select the file to be restored from the list by clicking on it with the mouse.

2) Click **File**.

3) Click **Restore**.

Viewing the Files in Different Orders

You may wish to view the contents of the Recycle Bin in a different order.

1) Click **View**.

2) Click **Details**.

3) Some headings will appear at the top of your list of files. When you click on them, the files will be sorted in that order.

Figure 13.4 - Details at the top of the list of files.

Name	Original Location	Date Deleted	Type	Size

Removing Individual Files Permanently

1) Select the file that you wish to remove permanently.

2) Click **File**, click **Delete**.

Emptying the Recycle Bin

1) You should only use this command if you are absolutely sure that you will never need any of the files again.

2) Click **File**. Click **Empty Recycle Bin**.

Chapter Fourteen

Microsoft® Word® for Windows®

This section was written for version 97, however in the main the
instructions are compatible with versions 6 and 7.

Getting Started

What is Microsoft Word?

Microsoft Word is a word processing package. It is used for typing documents such as letters and reports.

Documents

Each file in Microsoft Word is known as a document.

Screen Layout

The *Menu Bar* appears at the top of the screen.

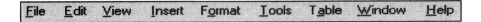

In addition to the menu bar, there are various *Buttons* on the screen.

Creating a New Document

Microsoft Word provides you with a blank document to type on when you launch the program. When you need another new document click the *New* icon, shown below. You will be provided with a blank screen to type on.

Saving Documents

Saving and Naming a Document

The first time that you save a document, you need to give it a name.

1) Click **File**.
2) Click **Save As**.
3) Type a name for the document in **File Name**.
4) Click **Save**.

Saving the Changes to a Document

Once you have saved the document for the first time and named it, you may need to make changes to it and re-save it. Use the following method for this:

1) Click **File**.
2) Click **Save**.

Using the Buttons

Click this button instead of **Save** or **Save As**.

The first time that you click the *Save* button in each workbook, the *Save As* screen will appear so that you can name the document. When you click this button after the worksheet has been named, the changes will be saved.

Opening Documents

Opening a Document

1)   Click **File**.
     Click **Open**.

2)   Look in the **File name** box for the file that you are trying to open, and click on
     it. (If it is not in there, you may need to refer to the section below on 'Opening
     a Document from Another Drive or Folder'.)

3)   Click **Open**.

Drives and Folders

For help in understanding the structure of drives and folders, see Chapters 5
and 9 before following the instructions below.

Opening a Document from Another Drive or Folder

1)   Click **File**, click **Open**.

2)   If the document is on another drive then click the drop down arrow to the right
     of the **File name** box and double click on the drive you need.

     If you can see your document at this point click on it, then click **Open**.

3)   To see the contents of a folder, double click on it in the **File name** box. A
     single folder may contain other folders. Double click on these to view their
     contents.

4)   Once you have found your document click on it.

5)   Click **Open**.

Copying and Moving Text

Copying Text

1) Select the text to be copied with the mouse.
2) Click **Edit**, click **Copy**.
3) Click the mouse at the point where the copy must appear.
4) Click **Edit**, click **Paste**.

Moving Text

1) Select the text to be moved with the mouse.
2) Click **Edit**, click **Cut**.
3) The text will disappear from the screen.
4) Click the cursor at the point where the text must reappear.
5) Click **Edit**, click **Paste**.

Using the Icons

1) Select the text to be moved or copied with the mouse.

   Use this button instead   Use this button instead
   of **Edit** and **Cut**.   of **Edit** and **Copy**.

2) Click at the point where you want the text to appear.

   Use this button instead
   of **Edit** and **Paste**.

Deleting

1) Drag the mouse over the text to be deleted.
2) Click **Edit,** click **Cut**, or press the <**Delete**> key on the keyboard.

For details on how to copy information to another file, see Chapter 4.

Tab Stops

Setting Tab Stops

1) Locate the ruler bar at the top of the document

Figure 14.1 - The ruler bar.

2) Single click the mouse on the ruler at the points where you would like your tab stops to be and markers will appear.

Figure 14.2 - Tab stops.

3) You can now use the **<Tab>** key on the keyboard (fourth key up on the left hand side of most keyboards) to jump to your tab stops in order to type lists of information.

Figure 14.3 - Using the tab stops.

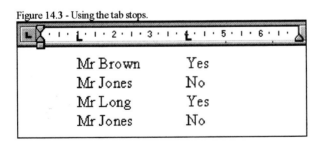

Moving / Deleting Tab Stops

1) Select lists that have been typed with the mouse.

2) Slide the tab stop along the ruler by clicking and dragging them with the mouse.

3) To delete a tab stop completely, drag it downwards off the ruler bar.

Decimal Tabs

Setting Decimal Tabs

1) Locate the tab stop sign at the far left hand side of the ruler bar.

2) Single click it three times so that it changes to this shape.

3) Now click the ruler at the point where you would like the decimal tabs to appear.

Figure 14.4 - Decimal tabs.

4) You can now type lists of information that line up on the decimal points.

Figure 14.5 - Using the decimal tabs.

200.00	300.00	500.00
1.00	2.00	3.00
30.00	20.00	40.00

Mix of Tab Stops

1) You can use different tab stops on the line at once.

2) Change the tab symbol before setting each one.

Figure 14.6 - Using a mix of tab stops.

Item One	200.00
Item Two	20.00
Item Three	300.00

Printing

Printing a Document

1) Click **File**.
2) Click **Print**.
3) Click **OK**.

Using the Icon

1) Click this icon.

2) This will send one copy of all the pages of your document to print.

Printing Multiple Copies

1) Click **File**.
2) Click **Print**.
3) Input the amount of copies required in the **Number of copies** box.
4) Click **OK**.

Printing Specific Pages

1) Click **File**.
2) Click **Print**.
3) In the **Pages** box, type in page numbers of the pages required, each one separated by a comma, e.g. **3,4,5**
   If a range is required, type the first and last page in the range e.g. **4-8**
4) Click **OK**.

Margins

To Change the Margins

1) Click **File**.
2) Click **Page Setup**.
3) Click **Margins**.
4) Look at the top of the dialogue box and make sure **Margins** is selected.
5) To alter your top margin, click in the **Top** box.
   To alter your bottom margin, click in the **Bottom** box.
   To alter your left margin, change the setting in the **Left** box.
   To alter your right margin, change the setting in the **Right** box.
6) Click **OK**.

Using the Ruler Bar

1) Locate the ruler bar at the top of the screen.

Figure 14.7 - Ruler bar.

2) Click **Edit** and **Select All**.

3) To move the right hand margin, drag this icon along the ruler with the mouse:

4) To move the left hand margin, drag this icon along the ruler with the mouse: (Use the bottom part of the icon.)

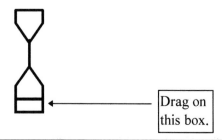

Drag on this box.

Fonts

Changing the Font Size

1) Select the text to be altered with the mouse.
2) Click the drop down arrow to the right of the following icon.
   `12 ▼`   When the list of sizes drops down, you will see a scroll bar on the right hand side of the list - use this to scroll to other sizes.
3) Select the size you want by clicking on the actual number.

Changing the Font Style

1) Select the text to be altered with the mouse.
2) Click the drop down arrow to the right of the following icon:
   `Times New Roman ▼`   When the list of fonts drops down, you will see a scroll bar on the right hand side of the list - use this to see even more fonts.
3) Select the font you want by clicking on its name.

Bold, Italics and Underline

1) Select the text to be altered with the mouse.
2) Select one or more of the following buttons:
   B Use for Bold.   *I* Use for Italic.   U Use for Underline.
3) To take one of the enhancements off, select the area to be altered and click the button again. Occasionally you may have to click the same button twice if you have selected a mixed area.

Alignment of Text

Centring Text

1) Select the text to be centred with the mouse.
2) Click the Centre button on the button bar.

Right Aligning Text

1) Select the text to be right aligned with the mouse.
2) Click the Align Right button on the button bar.

Left Aligning Text

1) Select the text to be left aligned with the mouse.
2) Click the Align Left button on the button bar.

Justify Text

1) Select the text to be justified with the mouse.
2) Click the Justify button on the button bar.

Indenting

What are Indents?

Indented text can be used for emphasis. Indented text wraps to a defined point.

Figure 14.8 - Indented text.

Indented Text ──────────────→

This text is not indented. It wraps to the left margin. This text is not indented. This text is not indented. This text is indented. It does not wrap to the left margin. This text is indented. It does not wrap to the left margin This text is not indented. It wraps to the left margin. This text is not indented. This text is not indented.

Using the Buttons

To indent a paragraph of text, click this button before you start to type it:

To take the indent off, click this button:

To insert or remove indents after you have typed a piece of text, select the text with the mouse and then click one of the buttons shown above.

Using the Keyboard

To indent a paragraph of text:

Press <**Ctrl**> and <**M**>.

To move paragraph back to the left hand margin:

Press <**Ctrl**> and <**Shift**> and <**M**>.

Hanging Indent

What are Hanging Indents?

A hanging indent indents all of the paragraph apart from the top line. This enables you to number the paragraph.

Figure 14.9 - Hanging indents.

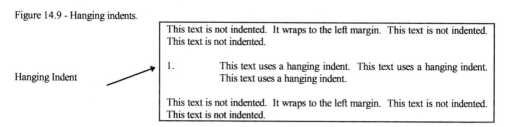

Hanging Indent

This text is not indented. It wraps to the left margin. This text is not indented. This text is not indented.

1.   This text uses a hanging indent. This text uses a hanging indent. This text uses a hanging indent.

This text is not indented. It wraps to the left margin. This text is not indented. This text is not indented.

Using the Keyboard

1) Type the paragraph number.
    Press the <Tab> key once.
    Press <Ctrl> and <T>.

    The indent marker will move along the ruler bar at the top of the screen to the position where the text will wrap.

    Figure 14.10 - The indent marker moves.

    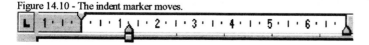

2) Type the paragraph of text. The indent will stay on for any subsequent paragraphs until you take it off.

3) To take it off:
    Press <Ctrl> and <Shift> and <T>.

Multi-levels of Text

What are Multi-levels?

Multi-levels of text are useful for sub-sections, as in this example:

Figure 14.11 - Multi-levels of numbering.

Multilevel indent

A meeting was held in December to discuss the following major points. Your comments are welcome.
1.　　　Building works will take place next winter. The following building will be repaired.
1.1　　　The workshop needs urgent attention. The workshop needs urgent attention.
This text is not indented. It wraps to the left margin. This text is not indented. This text is not indented.

Setting the Points

Place some tab stops on the ruler bar at the point where you would like the text to be indented to.

Figure 14.12 - Preparing the ruler bar.

Using Hanging Indents

1)　Press **<Ctrl>** and **<T>** to increase each indent.

The indent marker on the ruler will move forward each time to the next tab stop.

Figure 14.13 - The indent marker moves.

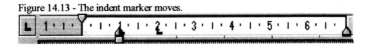

2)　Press **<Ctrl>** and **<Shift>** and **<T>** to decrease each indent.

Standard Paragraphs

Creating a Standard Paragraph

1) Type a paragraph of text, e.g. Thank you for your time on the telephone today.

2) Highlight it with the mouse.

3) Click **Insert**, click **Autotext**, click **New**.

4) In the **Please name your Autotext entry** box type a name for your standard paragraph, e.g. 'Thank'.

5) Click **OK**.

Retrieving a Standard Paragraph

1) Click **Insert**, click **Autotext**, click **Autotext**.

2) Select your paragraph from the list.

3) Click **Insert**.

Retrieving a Standard Paragraph with the Keyboard

1) Type the name of the standard paragraph.

2) Press the <F3> key on the keyboard directly after typing the name.
Your standard paragraph will pop out.

Mail Merge - I

What is Mail Merge?

Mail Merge enables you to combine a standard (*Form*) letter with a file of names and addresses, thus producing, simply and quickly, a batch of personalised letters.

The Stages

There are three stages to performing a Mail Merge. The details of how to execute each one are given in the next few pages.

1) The first stage is to create a datafile. This will usually be a file of names and addresses.

2)
1st February 1998
{{Company}}
{{Street}}
{{Town}}
{{County}}
Dear Sirs,
Please find enclosed...

The second stage is to create a standard letter (known as a form letter). Wherever a piece of personalised information is to appear you insert a field heading.

3) The third stage is to combine the standard letter with the datafile to produce personalised documents.

1st February 1998	1st February 1998	1st February 1998
Jones Ltd	Short Ltd	Browns Ltd
6 High Street	9 Shore Hill	6 Skylarks
Brighton	Hove	Crawley
Sussex	Sussex	Sussex
Dear Sirs,	Dear Sirs,	Dear Sirs,
Please find enclosed...	Please find enclosed...	Please find enclosed...

Mail Merge - II

Creating your Data File

1) Click **Tools**, click **Mail Merge**.

2) The Data Source box is not available until something has been selected in the *Form Letters* box, so click **Create**, click **Form Letters**, click **New Main Document**.

3) In Data Source, click **Get Data**, click **Create Data Source**.

4) Microsoft Word provides certain pre-defined fields: these are shown in the box entitled **Field names in header row**. To remove these, click **Remove Field Name** until they have all disappeared.

5) You now need to decide on the field headings that you require. A typical datafile might consist of the following fields.

   COMPANY - To store the name of the company.
   STREET - To store the first line of their address.
   TOWN - To store the name of the town that they are in.
   COUNTY - To store the name of the county they are in.
   POSTCODE - To store their postcode.

   Type the first field heading COMPANY in the **Field Name** box.
   Click **Add Field Name.**
   Enter all the rest of the headings in this way.

6) Click **OK** when you have finished and give your data file a name. Click **Save**.

7) Click **Edit Data Source**.

8) You can now enter your data. Press **<Enter>** to confirm each entry. When you get to the end of the record, a new blank one will appear.

9) When you have finished, click **OK**.

Mail Merge - III

Creating the Form Letter

You should now be able to see the merge toolbar on the screen.

Figure 14.14 - The mail merge toolbar.

Type your standard letter. Whenever you want to put in one of the fields from your data file, click the Insert Field button shown below.

Figure 14.15 - Inserting a field.

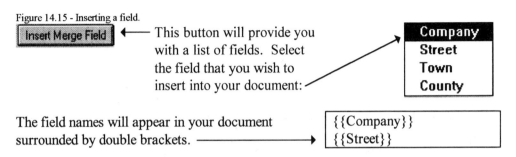

Insert Merge Field ◄—— This button will provide you with a list of fields. Select the field that you wish to insert into your document:

> Company
> Street
> Town
> County

The field names will appear in your document surrounded by double brackets. ————►

{{Company}}
{{Street}}

Merging the Form Letter with the Data File

1)   Make sure that you still have the form letter on the screen.

2)   Click **Tools**, click **Mail Merge**, click **Merge**.

3)   In **Merge To** select either **New Document** or **Printer**.

4)   Click **Merge**.

Using the Buttons

Once you have created your form letter, you could use the following buttons.

 This button will merge the documents onto the screen.

 This button will merge the documents and print them.

Chapter Fifteen

Lotus® WordPro® for Windows®

This section was written for the 96 Edition, however in the main the instructions are compatible with the 97 Edition.

Getting Started

What is WordPro?

Lotus WordPro is a word processing package. It is used for typing documents such as letters and reports.

Documents

Each file in WordPro is called a document.

Screen Layout

The *Menu Bar* appears at the top of the screen.

In addition to the menu bar there are various *Smart Icons* on the screen.

Creating New Documents

1)   Launch WordPro. Click **Create a Plain Document**.

2)   If WordPro is already running, then click the following icon:

Click **Create a Plain Document**.

3)   You will be provided with a blank screen to type on.

Saving Documents

Saving and Naming a Document

The first time that you save a document, you need to give it a name.

1) Click **File**.
2) Click **Save As**.
3) Type a name for the document in **File name**.
4) Click **Save**.

Saving the Changes to a Document

Once you have saved the document for the first time and named it, you may need to make changes to it and re-save it. Use the following method for this:

1) Click **File**.
2) Click **Save**.

Using the Buttons

Click this button instead of **Save** or **Save As**.

The first time that you click the *Save* button in each workbook, the *Save As* screen will appear so that you can name the document. When you click this button after the worksheet has been named, the changes will be saved.

Opening Documents

Opening a Document

1) Click **File**.
   Click **Open**.

2) Look in the **File Name** box for the file that you are trying to open, and click on it. (If it is not in there, you may need to refer to the section below on 'Opening a Document from Another Drive or Directory'.)

3) Click **OK**.

Drives and Directories

For help in understanding the structure of drives and directories see Chapter 6 before following the instructions below.

Opening a Document from Another Drive or Directory

1) Click **File**, click **Open**.

2) If the document is on another drive, then click the drop down arrow to the right of the **Drives** box and click on the drive that you need.

   If you can see your document at this point click on it, then click **OK**.

3) To see the contents of a folder, double click on it in the **Directories** box. A single folder may contain other folders, so double click on these to view their contents.

4) Once you have found your document, click on it.

5) Click **OK**.

Copying and Moving Text

Copying Text

1) Select the text to be copied with the mouse.
2) Click **Edit**, click **Copy**.
3) Click the mouse at the point where the copy must appear.
4) Click **Edit**, click **Paste**.

Moving Text

1) Select the text to be moved with the mouse.
2) Click **Edit**, click **Cut**.
3) The text will disappear from the screen.
4) Click the cursor at the point where the text must reappear.
5) Click **Edit**, click **Paste**.

Using the Smart Icons

1) Select the text to be moved or copied with the mouse.

Use this button instead of **Edit** and **Cut**:   Use this button instead of **Edit** and **Copy**:

2) Click at the point where you want the text to appear.

Click this button instead of **Edit** and **Paste**:

Deleting

1) Drag the mouse over the text to be deleted.
2) Click **Edit,** click **Cut**, or press the **<Delete>** key on the keyboard.

For details on how to copy information to another file, see Chapter 4.

Tab Stops

Setting Tab Stops

1) Make sure that the ruler bar is showing at the top of the document. If it is not then click **View**, click **Show/Hide,** click **Ruler**.

Figure 15.1 - The ruler bar.

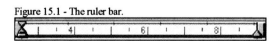

2) Single click the mouse on the ruler at the points where you would like your tab stops to be and markers will appear - as shown below.

Figure 15.2 - Placing tab stops on the ruler bar.

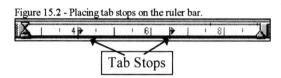

3) You can now use the **<Tab>** key on the keyboard (fourth key up on the left hand side) to jump to your tab stops in order to type lists of information.

Figure 15.3 - Lists created using tab stops.

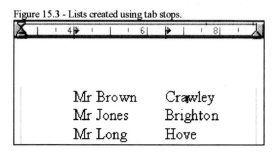

Moving / Deleting Tab Stops

1) Select the lists that have been typed with the mouse.

2) Click and drag the tab stop along the ruler.

3) To delete a tab stop completely, click and drag it downwards off the ruler bar.

Numeric Tabs

Setting Decimal Tabs

1) Click the ruler bar with the *Right Hand* mouse button. A menu of all the tab settings will appear.

2) Click **Create Numeric Tabs**.

3) Click the ruler bar at the points where you would like your decimal tab to appear.

Figure 15.4 - Decimal tabs.

Decimal Tab

4) You can now type lists of information that line up on the decimal point.

Figure 15.5 - Mixed tab stops.

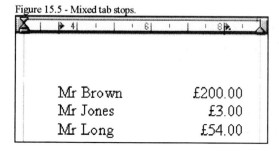

Mr Brown	£200.00
Mr Jones	£3.00
Mr Long	£54.00

Printing

Printing a Document

1) Click **File**.
2) Click **Print**.
3) Click **Print**.

Using the Icon

1) Click this icon.

2) This will send one copy of all the pages of your document to print.

Printing Multiple Copies

1) Click **File**.
2) Click **Print**.
3) Input the number of copies required in the **Copies** box.
4) Click **Print**.

Printing Specific Pages

1) Click **File**.
2) Click **Print**.
3) Click **Pages**. In the **List the pages box** type in the numbers of the pages required, each one separated by a comma, e.g. **3,4,5**
   If a range is required, type the first and last page in the range, e.g. **4-8**
4) Click **Print**.

Margins

To Change the Margins

1) Click **File**.

2) Click **Document Properties**.

3) Click **Page**.

4) To alter your top margin, click in the **Top** box.
    To alter your bottom margin, click in the **Bottom** box.
    To alter your left margin, change the setting in the **Left** box.
    To alter your right margin, change the setting in the **Right** box.

5) Click the *Close* **X**.

Using the Ruler Bar

1) Look for the ruler bar at the top of the screen. If it is not showing, click **View**, click **Show/Hide**. Click **Ruler**.

Figure 15.6 - The ruler bar.

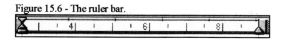

2) Click **Edit** and **Select All**.

3) Now click and drag the left and right markers to alter the left and right margins.

Figure 15.7 - The margin markers.

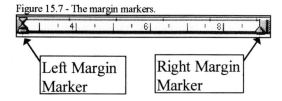

Left Margin Marker   Right Margin Marker

Fonts

Changing the Font Size

1) Select the text to be altered with the mouse.
2) Click **Text**, click **Font & Color**.
3) Click the **AZ** tag.
4) Select the **Size**.
5) Click the *Close* **X**.

Changing the Font Name

1) Select the text to be altered with the mouse.
2) Click **Text**, click **Font & Colour**.
3) Click the **AZ** tag.
4) Select the **Font Name**.
5) Click the *Close* **X**.

Using the Icons

These icons are located in the bottom left hand corner of the screen. If the last font name and font size to be selected was not *Times New Roman* and *12* then the buttons may have different wording on them.

Use this icon to change the Font Name:    Use this icon to change the font size.

Bold, Italics and Underline

1) Select the text to be altered on the mouse.

2) Click this button to cycle through the options for Bold, Italic and Underline.

Alignment of Text

How to Align Text

1) Select the text to be re-aligned with the mouse.
2) Use this button to cycle through the alignment options.

Alignment Examples

Left Aligned

Mr Brown
Mr Long
Mr Jones

Left-aligned text extends from the left hand margin. It is the default setting.

Right Aligned

1st February 1998

Right-aligned text extends from the right hand margin. It is useful for typing dates.

Centred

Jones & Son
Annual Report

Centred text puts all the text in the middle of the screen. It is useful for typing titles.

Justified

This text is evenly spaced between the left and right margins.

Justified text hangs evenly between the left and right margins, making the text look straight on each edge.

Standard Paragraphs

Creating Standard Paragraphs

1) Type a paragraph of text.

2) Highlight it with the mouse.

3) Click **Edit**.

4) Click **Glossary**.

5) Type in a name for your paragraph in **Glossary entry name**.

6) Click the **Create** button.

To Use a Standard Paragraph

Method One

1) Place the cursor where you would like the paragraph to appear.

2) Click **Edit** then **Glossary**.

3) Select the name of the paragraph. Click the **Insert** button.

Method Two

1) Place the cursor where you would like the paragraph to appear.

2) Type the glossary name.

3) Hold down the <**Ctrl**> key and press <**K**>.

Mail Merge - I

What is Mail Merge?

Mail Merge enables you to combine a standard letter with a file of names and addresses, thus producing, simply and quickly, a batch of personalised letters.

The Stages

There are three stages to performing a Mail Merge. The details of how to execute each one are given in the next few pages.

1)   The first stage is to create a datafile. This will usually be a file of names and addresses.

2)
1st February 1998
<Company>   <Street>   <Town>   <County>
Dear Sirs,
Please find enclosed...

The second stage is to create a standard letter. Wherever a piece of personalised information is to appear, you insert a field heading.

3)   The third stage is to combine the standard letter with the datafile to produce personalised documents.

1st February 1998	1st February 1998	1st February 1998
Jones Ltd 6 High Street Brighton Sussex	Short Ltd 9 Shore Hill Hove Sussex	Browns Ltd 6 Skylarks Crawley Sussex
Dear Sirs,	Dear Sirs,	Dear Sirs,
Please find enclosed...	Please find enclosed...	Please find enclosed...

Mail Merge - II

Create the DataFile

1) Click **Text**.

2) Click **Merge**.

3) The *Merge Assistant* will appear.

4) Click **New DataFile**.

5) Enter the name of the first field that you require in **Field name**, e.g. COMPANY.
Click **Add** and it will appear in the **Fields** section.

   Repeat this step for each field that you require.

6) Once you have set up all of your fields, click **OK**.

7) The *Edit DataFile* screen will appear.

8) Type in the first address. Use **<Tab>** to get from box to box.
Click **Add Record** when you have completed the first address.
Click **New Record** to enter the next one.

   Repeat this process until you have inserted all of the addresses.

9) Click **Close File**.

10) Click **Yes** to save the changes.

11) Give the file a name and click **OK**.

Mail Merge - III

Creating the Standard Letter

1) Once you have created the data file, the *Merge Assistant* will appear on the screen again.

2) Click **Next**.

3) Click **Insert Merge Fields**.

4) A blank screen will appear so that you can type your letter. You will also see a list of your fields at the top of the screen.

Figure 15.8 - The list of fields.

5) Type the letter as normal. When ever you need a field select it from the list of fields and then click the **Insert Field** button.

Merging the Data File with the Letter

1) Once you have finished typing your letter, click **Done**.

2) The *Merge Assistant* will reappear. Click **Done**.

3) A merged version of the first letter will appear on the screen, together with some extra buttons which you can use to either print or view this document and the subsequent ones.

Figure 15.9 - Print and view buttons.

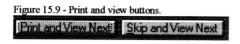

4) To see the next letter, click **Skip and View Next**.
    To print this letter, click **Print and View Next**.
    To print all of the merged letters, click **Print All**.

Chapter Sixteen

Corel® WordPerfect® for Windows® v7

This section was written for version 7.

Getting Started

What is WordPerfect?

Corel WordPerfect is a word processing package. It is used for typing documents such as letters and reports.

Screen Layout

The *Menu Bar* appears at the top of the screen.

In addition to the menu bar there are various *Buttons* on the screen.

Creating a New Document

WordPerfect provides you with a new document to work on as soon as it is launched. A new document is also provided when you close down any open documents that you have on the screen. Should you require new documents at any other time, then click on the *New Document* button shown below. You will be provided with a blank screen on which to type information.

Saving Documents

Saving and Naming Documents

The first time that you save a document you need to give it a name.

1) Click **File**.
2) Click **Save As**.
3) Type a name for the document in **Name**.
4) Click **Save**.

Saving the Changes to a Document

Once you have saved the document for the first time and named it, you may need to make changes to it and re-save it. Use the following method for this.

1) Click **File**.
2) Click **Save**.

Using the Buttons

Click this button instead of **Save** or **Save As**.

The first time that you click the *save* button in each workbook, the *Save As* screen will appear so that you can name the document. When you click this button after the worksheet has been named, the changes will be saved.

Opening Documents

Opening a Document

1) Click **File**.
    Click **Open**.

2) Look at the list of files for the file that you are trying to open, and click on it.
    (If it is not in there, you may need to refer to the section below on 'Opening a
    Document from Another Drive or Folder'.)

3) Click **Open**.

Drives and Folders

For help in understanding the structure of drives and folders, see Chapters 5
and 9 before following the instructions below.

Opening a Document from Another Drive or Folder

1) Click **File**, click **Open**.

2) If the document is on another drive then click the drop down arrow to the right
    of the **Look in** box and double click on the drive you need.

    If you can see your document at this point click on it, then click **Open**.

3) To see the contents of a folder, double click on it in the **Look in** box. A single
    folder may contain other folders so double click on these to view their contents.

4) Once you have found your document, click on it.

5) Click **Open**.

Copying and Moving Text

Copying Text

1) Select the text to be copied with the mouse.
2) Click **Edit**, click **Copy**.
3) Click the mouse at the point where the copy must appear.
4) Click **Edit**, click **Paste**.

Moving Text

1) Select the text to be moved with the mouse.
2) Click **Edit**, click **Cut**.
3) The text will disappear from the screen.
4) Click the cursor at the point where the text must reappear.
5) Click **Edit**, click **Paste**.

Using the Icons

1) Select the text to be moved or copied with the mouse.

Use this button instead of **Edit** and **Cut**. Use this button instead of **Edit** and **Copy**.

2) Click at the point where you want the text to appear.

Use this button instead of **Edit** and **Paste**.

Deleting

1) Drag the mouse over the text to be deleted.
2) Click **Edit,** click **Cut,** or press the <Delete> key on the keyboard.

For details on how to copy information to another file, see Chapter 4.

Tab Stops - I

Locate the Ruler Bar

1) You may need to bring the ruler bar up onto the screen.

Click **View.**
Click **Toolbars/Ruler.**
Click in the ruler bar check box.
Click **OK.**

There are markers on the ruler bar that depict the position of the default tab stops.

Figure 16.1 - Default tab stops.

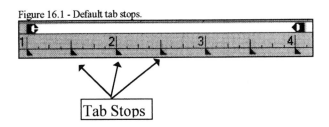

Tab Stops

2) To jump to each tab stop, use the **<Tab>** key on the keyboard.

3) You will then be able to create lists similar to those shown below.

Figure 16.2 - Using the default tab stops.

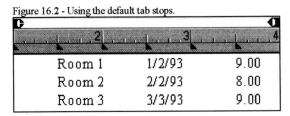

Room 1	1/2/93	9.00
Room 2	2/2/93	8.00
Room 3	3/3/93	9.00

Tab Stops - II

Clearing the Default Tab Stops

1) Before creating your tab stops you will need to clear the default tab stops.

2) Click **Format**.
3) Click **Line**.
4) Click **Tab Set**.

5) Click **Clear All**.
6) Click **OK**.

Setting Tab Stops

1) Click the mouse on the ruler bar at the position you require.

2) A marker will appear on the ruler bar at that point.

Figure 16. 3 - Setting tab stops.

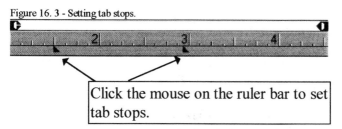

Click the mouse on the ruler bar to set tab stops.

3) To jump to the various tab stops, press the **<Tab>** key on the keyboard.

Figure 16.4 - A list created after setting tab stops.

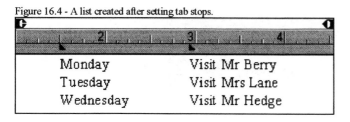

Monday	Visit Mr Berry
Tuesday	Visit Mrs Lane
Wednesday	Visit Mr Hedge

Tab Stops - III

What are Decimal Tabs?

Decimal tabs are tabs which align information on the decimal point.

Figure 16.5 - Using decimal tabs.

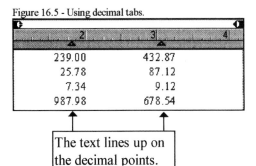

The text lines up on
the decimal points.

Setting Decimal Tabs

1) Clear all the default tab stops.

2) Hover the mouse over the lowest level of the ruler bar and click the *right-hand* mouse button.

3) Click **Decimal**.

4) Click the mouse on the ruler at the points where you wish the tab stops to appear. The decimal tab stop markers will appear. However, they will be a different shape to the normal left align tab stop.

Figure 16.6 - Decimal tab stops.

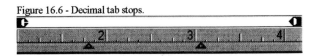

5) To jump to the various tab stops, press the **<Tab>** key on the keyboard.

Printing

Printing a Document

1) Click **File**.
2) Click **Print**.
3) Click **Print**.

Using the Icon

1) Click this
   icon.

2) This will send one copy of all the pages of your document to print.

Printing Multiple Copies

1) Click **File**.
2) Click **Print**.
3) Input the number of copies required in the **Number of copies** box.
4) Click **Print**.

Printing Specific Pages

1) Click **File**.
2) Click **Print**.
3) In the **Page range** section, type the first page number to be printed in **from** and the last page to be printed in **to**.
4) Click **Print**.

Margins

To Change the Margins

1) Click **Format**.
2) Click **Margins**.
3) To alter your left margin, change the setting in the **Left** box.
   To alter your right margin, change the setting in the **Right** box.
   To alter your top margin, click in the **Top** box.
   To alter your bottom margin, click in the **Bottom** box.
4) Click **OK**.

Displaying the Ruler Bar

1) The ruler bar should be displayed at the top of the screen. If you cannot see it then follow the steps in this section.

Figure 16.7 - The ruler bar.

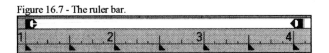

2) Click **View**, click **Toolbars/Ruler**.
   Click in the ruler bar check box, click **OK**.

Changing the Margins Using the Ruler Bar

1) Make sure that the ruler bar is showing.

2) Click and drag on the margin markers. It is important to click and drag on exactly the right point on the markers.

Figure 16. 8 - The margin markers.

| Click on the left hand side of the marker to adjust the left margin. | Click on the right hand side of the marker to adjust the right margin. |

Fonts

Changing the Font Size

1) Select the text to be altered with the mouse.

2) Click the drop down arrow to the right of the following icon.

3) Select the size you want by clicking on the actual number.

Changing the Font Style

1) Select the text to be altered with the mouse.

2) Click the drop down arrow to the right of the following icon.

3) Select the font you want by clicking on its name.

Bold, Italics and Underline

1) Select the text to be altered with the mouse.

2) Select one or more of the following buttons:

 Use for Bold.   Use for Italic.   Use for Underline.

3) To take one of the enhancements off, select the area to be altered and click the button again. Occasionally you may have to click the same button twice if you have selected a mixed area.

The Edit Button

Displaying the Edit Button

1) Type a piece of text.

> Thank you for your time on the
> telephone today. As promised I
> am enclosing our brochure.

2) Move the mouse back over the text and a button will appear to the left of the top row of the paragraph.

Figure 16.9 - The *Edit* button

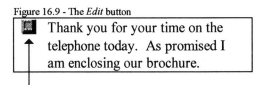

> Thank you for your time on the
> telephone today. As promised I
> am enclosing our brochure.

The Edit Button

3) Click on the Edit Button and the following menu will be displayed. The following section requires the use of the *Paragraph Menu*.

Figure 16.10 - The paragraph menu.

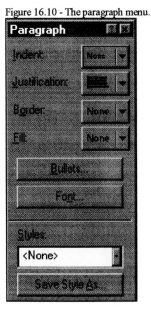

Justification

1) Type a piece of text.

2) Hover over it with the mouse.

3) Click the Edit Button that appears to the left of the first line of the paragraph.

4) Select **<u>J</u>ustification** and a box with choices in it will appear.

5) This button is the default. When it is selected, text will be aligned on the left hand side of the page.

Example of left-aligned text. Example of left-aligned text. Example of left-aligned text.

This button will align text on the right hand side of the page.

Example of right-aligned text. Example of right-aligned text. Example of right-Aligned text.

This button centres the text in the middle of the page.

Example of centred text

This button will justify the text so that it is straight down both the right hand and left hand edges of the page.

This is justified text. This is justified text. This is justified text. This is justified text.

Indenting

What are Indents?

Indented text can be used for emphasis. Indented text wraps to a defined point.

Figure 16.11 - Indented text

Indented text   ───────────────────▶

> This text is not indented. It wraps to the left margin. This text is not indented. This text is not indented.
>
> This text is indented. It does not wrap to the left margin. This text is indented. It does not wrap to the left margin.
>
> This text is not indented. It wraps to the left margin. This text is not indented. This text is not indented.

Creating an Indent

1)   Click the *right-hand* mouse button.

2)   Choose **Indent**.

3)   The cursor will jump to a point slightly to the right of the left-hand margin.

4)   Type a paragraph of text. When the text wraps, it will indent.

5)   When you have finished typing the indented paragraph, press **<Enter>** on the keyboard and your cursor will go back to the left-hand margin.

6)   If you wish to indent another paragraph, then repeat the above process.

Standard Paragraphs

Creating a Standard Paragraph

1) Type a paragraph of text, e.g. Thank you for your time on the telephone today.

2) Highlight it with the mouse.

3) Click **Insert**.
   Click **Abbreviations**.
   Click **Create**.

4) Type an **Abbreviation Name**.
   e.g. Thank.
   (Start the abbreviation name with a capital letter.)

5) Click **OK**.
   Click **Close**.

Using an Abbreviation

1) Click **Insert**.
   Click **Abbreviations**.

2) Select the abbreviation.
   Click **Expand**.

Using the Keyboard to Retrieve an Abbreviation

1) Type the name of the abbreviation, e.g. Thank.

2) Press <Ctrl> and <A> on the keyboard directly after the name of the abbreviation. The abbreviation should pop out.

Mail Merge - I

What is Mail Merge?

Mail Merge enables you to combine a standard (*Form*) letter with a file of names and addresses, thus producing, simply and quickly, a batch of personalised letters.

The Stages

There are three stages to performing a Mail Merge. The details of how to execute each one are given in the next few pages.

1) The first stage is to create a datafile. This will usually be a file of names and addresses.

2)
```
1st February 1998

FIELD(Company)
FIELD(Street)
FIELD(Town)
FIELD(County)

Dear Sirs,

Please find enclosed...
```
The second stage is to create a standard letter (known as a form letter). Wherever a piece of personalised information is to appear, you insert a field heading.

3) The third stage is to combine the standard letter with the datafile to produce personalised documents.

```
1st February 1998

Jones Ltd
6 High Street
Brighton
Sussex

Dear Sirs,

Please find enclosed...
```

```
1st February 1998

Short Ltd
9 Shore Hill
Hove
Sussex

Dear Sirs,

Please find enclosed...
```

```
1st February 1998

Browns Ltd
6 Skylarks
Crawley
Sussex

Dear Sirs,

Please find enclosed...
```

Mail Merge - II

Creating your DataFile

1)   Click **Tools**, click **Merge**, click **Data File**.

2)   You now need to decide on the field headings that you require. A typical datafile might consist of the following fields.

COMPANY - To store the name of the company.
STREET - To store the first line of their address.
TOWN - To store the name of the town that they are in.
COUNTY - To store the name of the county they are in.
POSTCODE - To store their postcode.

Type the first field heading COMPANY in the **Name a Field**.
Click **Add** to confirm it.

Enter all the rest of the headings in this way.
Click **OK**.

3)   You are now in the *quick data entry form*.
Enter the details of your customers. Use the **<Enter>** key on the keyboard to confirm each entry and take you to the next box. Press the **<Enter>** key on the last field and a new blank form will come into view.

4)   When you have entered the last address, click **Close**.

5)   Click **Yes** to save your changes to disk. Give your data file a name in the **Name** box and click **Save**.

6)   Click **File**, click **Close**.

Mail Merge - III

Creating the Form Letter

1) Click **Tools**, click **Merge**, click **Form**.

2) Click **New Document Window**, click **OK**.

3) Select your datafile by clicking the icon to the right of the **'Associate a Data File'** box. Choose your datafile from the list. Click **Select**. Click **OK**.

4) You should now be able to see the *merge button bar* on the screen. Type your standard letter. Whenever you want to put in one of the fields from your datafile, click the **Insert Field** button on the *merge button bar*.

Insert Field...

5) After you have clicked the Insert Field button, a list of fields will pop up.

   Select the one that you want.

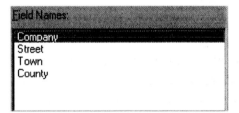

Field Names:

Company
Street
Town
County

6) Click the **Insert** button.

7) The field name will appear in your document.

FIELD(Company)

8) Click **Close**.

9) Repeat steps 4-8 for every field that you wish to include.

Merging the Form Letter with the Data File

1) With the form letter still open, click the **Merge** button.

2) Click **Merge**.

Chapter Seventeen

Corel® WordPerfect® for Windows® v8

This section was written for version 8.

Getting Started

What is WordPerfect?

WordPerfect is a word processing package. It is used for typing documents such as letters and reports.

Screen Layout

The *Menu Bar* appears at the top of the screen.

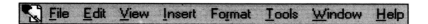

In addition to the menu bar there are various *buttons*.

Creating New Documents

WordPerfect automatically provides you with a blank document when you launch the package or close the document that you are currently working on. However, should you still need to create a new document click on the *New Document* button shown below. You will be provided with a blank screen to type on.

Saving Documents

To Save a Document

1) Click **File**.
2) Click **Save As**.
3) Give the document a name in the **File name** box, Click **Save**.

Drives and Folders

For help understanding the structure of drives and folders, see the sections on Drives and Directories in Chapter 9 before following the instructions below.

Saving the Document to Another Directory or Drive

1) If you wish to save the document on another drive then click the drop down arrow to the right of the **Save in** box, and double click on the drive you need. Click **Save**.

2) If you wish to save the document in another folder, double click on the name of the folder in the **Save in** box. A single folder may contain other folders, so double click on these to find the folder that you wish to use. Click **Save**.

Saving the Changes to a Document

Click **File,** click **Save**.

Using the Buttons

Click this button instead of **Save** or **Save As**.

The first time that you click the *Save* button in each workbook, the *Save As* screen will appear so that you can name the document. When you click this button after the worksheet has been named, the changes will be saved.

Opening Documents

Opening a Document

1) Click **File**.
   Click **Open**.

2) Look in the main box for the file that you are trying to open, and click on it. (If it is not in there, you may need to refer to the section below on 'Opening a Document from Another Drive or Folder'.)

3) Click **Open**.

Drives and Folders

For help in understanding the structure of drives and folders, see Chapters 5 and 9 before following the instructions below.

Opening a Document from Another Drive or Folder

1) Click **File**, click **Open**.

2) If the document is on another drive then click the drop down arrow to the right of the **Look in** box and double click on the drive you need.

   If you can see your document at this point click on it, then click **Open**.

3) If the document is in another folder, double click on the name of the folder in the **Look in** box. A single folder may contain other folders, so double click on these to view their contents.

4) Once you have found your document, click on it.

5) Click **Open**.

Copying and Moving Text

Copying Text

1) Select the text to be copied with the mouse.
2) Click **Edit**, click **Copy**.
3) Click the mouse at the point where the copy must appear.
4) Click **Edit**, click **Paste**.

Moving Text

1) Select the text to be moved with the mouse.
2) Click **Edit**, click **Cut**.
3) The text will disappear from the screen.
4) Click the cursor at the point where the text must reappear.
5) Click **Edit**, click **Paste**.

Using the Icons

1) Select the text to be moved or copied with the mouse.

Use this button instead of **Edit** and **Cut**.   Use this button instead of **Edit** and **Copy**.

2) Click at the point where you want the text to appear.

Use this button instead of **Edit** and **Paste**.

Deleting

1) Drag the mouse over the text to be deleted.
2) Click **Edit,** click **Cut**, or press the <Delete> key on the keyboard.

For details on how to copy information to another file, see Chapter 4.

Tab Stops - I

Locate the Ruler Bar

1) You may need to bring the ruler bar up onto the screen.

    Click **V**iew.
    Click **R**uler.

    There are markers on the ruler bar that depict the position of the default tab stops.

Figure 17.1 - Default tab stops.

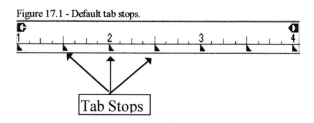

Tab Stops

2) To jump to each tab stop, use the **<Tab>** key on the keyboard.

3) You can now create lists similar to those shown below.

Figure 17.2 - Using the default tab stops.

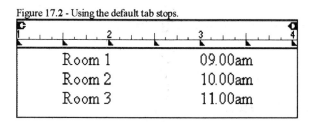

Room 1	09.00am
Room 2	10.00am
Room 3	11.00am

Tab Stops - II

Clearing the Default Tab Stops

1) Before creating your tab stops you will need to clear the default tab stops.

2) Click **Format**.
3) Click **Line**.
4) Click **Tab Set**.

5) Click **Clear All**.
6) Click **OK**.

Setting Tab Stops

1) Click the mouse on the ruler bar at the position you require.

2) A marker will appear on the ruler bar at that point.

Figure 17.3 - Setting tab stops.

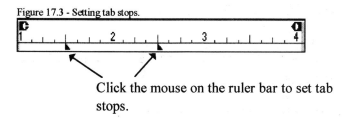

Click the mouse on the ruler bar to set tab stops.

3) To jump to the various tab stops, press the **<Tab>** key on the keyboard.

Figure 17.4 - A list created after setting tab stops.

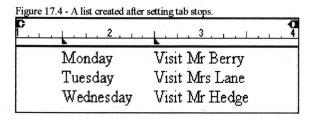

Tab Stops - III

What are Decimal Tabs?

Decimal tabs are tabs which align information on the decimal point.

Figure 17.5 - Using decimal tabs.

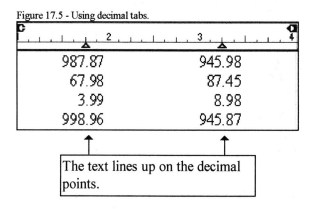

The text lines up on the decimal points.

Setting Decimal Tabs

1)   Clear all the default tab stops.

2)   Hover the mouse over the ruler bar and click the *right-hand* mouse button.

3)   Click **Decimal**.

4)   Click the mouse on the ruler at the points where you wish the tab stops to appear. The decimal tab stop markers will appear. However, they will be a different shape from the normal left align tab stop.

Figure 17. 6 - Decimal tab stops.

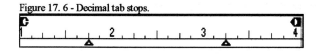

5)   To jump to the various tab stops while you are typing, press the **<Tab>** key on the keyboard.

Tab Stops - IV

Mixed Tab Stops

You can use a mix of different tab stops on the ruler at the same time.

Figure 17. 7 - Using mixed tab stops.

Paint	78.98
Wallpaper	234.88
Accessories	8.45
Furniture	876.98

1) Clear all existing default tab stops off the ruler bar.

2) Hover over the ruler bar and select the type of tab stop that you require, e.g. **Left**. Click the mouse on the ruler bar at the desired position.

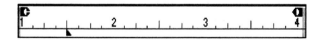

3) To change the type of tab stop that you are putting onto the ruler bar, click the *right-hand* mouse button over the ruler and select another type, e.g. **Decimal**.

4) Click the mouse at the points where the tabs are to appear.

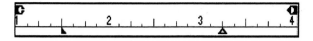

Tab Stops - V

What is a Dot Leader Tab Stop?

A dot leader tab displays a line of dots between the previous tab stop and itself.

Figure 17. 8 - A dot leader tab stop.

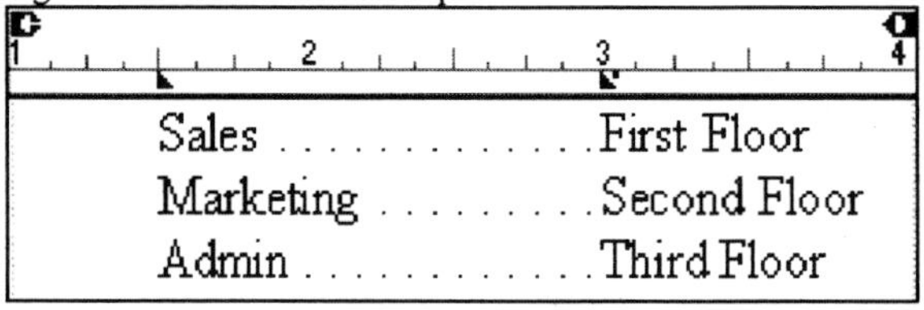

```
Sales . . . . . . . . . . . . First Floor
Marketing . . . . . . . . Second Floor
Admin . . . . . . . . . . Third Floor
```

You can also choose to have a decimal dot leader tab stop.

Figure 17.9 - Decimal dot leader tab stop.

```
America . . . . . . . . £500.00
Canada  . . . . . . . . £460.00
Australia . . . . . . . . £700.00
```

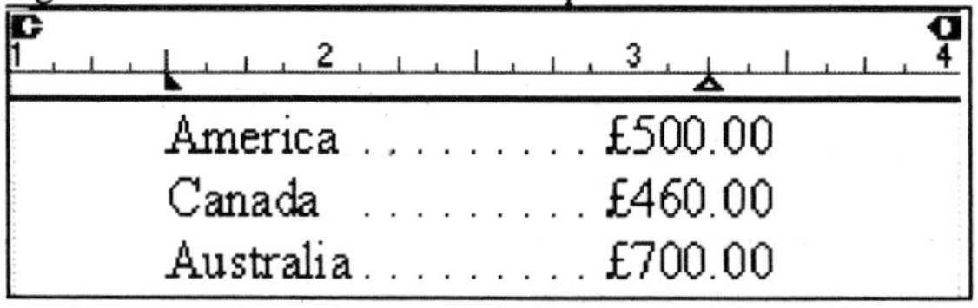

Creating a Dot Leader Tab Stop

1) Clear all existing tab stops from the line and set a normal left tab stop at the position that you require for the first column.

2) Hover over the ruler with the mouse and click the *right-hand* mouse button. A menu will appear. Click **...Left** or **...Decimal**.

3) The dots will not appear until you actually use the tab stops to create your lists.

Printing

Printing a Document

1) Click **File**.
2) Click **Print**.
3) Click **Print**.

Using the Icon

1) Click this
   icon.

2) This will send one copy of all the pages of your document to print.

Printing Multiple Copies

1) Click **File**.
2) Click **Print**.
3) Input the number of copies required in the **Number of Copies** box.
4) Click **OK**.

Printing Specific Pages

1) Click **File**.
2) Click **Print**.
3) In the **Print pages** boxes, enter the page number of the first page to be printed and the last page to be printed.
4) Click **Print**.

Margins

To Change the Margins

1) Click **Format**.
2) Click **Margins**.
3) To alter your left margin, change the setting in the **Left** box.
    To alter your right margin, change the setting in the **Right** box.
    To alter your top margin, click in the **Top** box.
    To alter your bottom margin, click in the **Bottom** box.

4) Click **OK**.

Displaying the Ruler Bar

1) The ruler bar should be displayed at the top of the screen. If you cannot see it then follow the steps in this section.

Figure 17.10 - The ruler bar.

2) Click **View**.
    Click **Ruler**.

Changing the Margins Using the Ruler Bar

1) Make sure that the ruler bar is showing.

2) Click and drag on the margin markers. It is important to click and drag on exactly the point on the markers.

Figure 17.11 - The margin markers.

| Click on the left hand side of the marker to adjust the left margin. | Click on the right hand side of the marker to adjust the right margin. |

Fonts

Changing the Font Size

1) Select the text to be altered with the mouse.

2) Click the drop down arrow to the right of the following icon.

3) Select the size you want by clicking on the actual number.

Changing the Font Style

1) Select the text to be altered with the mouse.

2) Click the drop down arrow to the right of the following icon.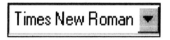

3) Select the font you want by clicking on its name.

Bold, Italics and Underline

1) Select the text to be altered on the mouse.

2) Select one or more of the following buttons.

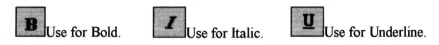

3) To take one of the enhancements off, simply select the area to be altered and click the button again. Occasionally you may have to click the same button twice if you have selected a mixed area.

Alignment of Text

1)   Select the text to be centred with the mouse.

2)   Click the centre button from the button bar.

3)   The following options will be displayed:

4)   This button is the default. When it is selected, text will be aligned on the left hand side of the page.

Example of left-aligned text. Example of left-aligned text. Example of left-aligned text.

This button will align text on the right hand side of the page.

Example of right-aligned text. Example of right-aligned text. Example of right-Aligned text.

This button centres the text in the middle of the page.

Example of centred text

This button will justify the text so that it is straight down both the right hand and left hand edges of the page.

This is justified text. This is justified text. This is justified text. This is justified text.

Indenting

What are Indents?

Indented text can be used for emphasis. Indented text wraps to a defined point.

Figure 17.12 - Indented text.

Indented Text ⎯⎯⎯⎯⎯⎯⎯⎯⎯⎯⎯➤

This text is not indented. It wraps to the left margin. This text is not indented. This text is not indented.

This text is indented. It does not wrap to the left margin. This text is indented. It does not wrap to the left margin

This text is not indented. It wraps to the left margin. This text is not indented. This text is not indented.

Creating an Indent

1) Click **Format**.
2) Click **Paragraph**.
3) Click **Indent**.
4) Your text will wrap to the indent.
5) When you press **<Enter>** on the keyboard, the cursor will go back to the left hand margin.

Using the Keyboard

1) Press **<F7>** on the keyboard.
2) Your text will wrap to the indent.
3) When you press **<Enter>** on the keyboard, the cursor will go back to the left hand margin.

Hanging Indents

What are Hanging Indents?

Hanging indents of text are useful for sub-sections, as in this example:

Figure 17.13 - Hanging indents.

Indented Text ───────────▶

A meeting was held in December to discuss the following major points. Your comments are welcome.
1.   Building works will take place next winter. The following building will be repaired.

Using QuickIndent

1) Type the paragraph number.

2) Press the <**Tab**> key on the keyboard. The text will continue to indent to this point until you press <**Enter**>, then the next sequential number will appear. Press <**Enter**> again to get a space.

3) To indent the text to the next level, press the <**Tab**> key on the keyboard.

    Type the paragraph number.

    Press the <**Tab**> key on the keyboard again. The text will continue to indent to this point until, you press <**Enter**>, then the next sequential number will appear. Press <**Enter**> again to get a space.

4) To resume typing without the indent, bring up the next number then click this button:

Standard Paragraphs

Creating an Abbreviation

1) Type a paragraph of text, e.g. Thank you for your time on the telephone today.

2) Highlight it with the mouse.

3) Click **Tools**.
   Click **Quickwords**.

4) Type a name for your abbreviation in the box labelled
   Abbreviated Form (type this Quickword in Document),
   e.g. Thank1.

5) Click **Add Entry**.

Retrieving an Abbreviation

1) Click **Tools**.
   Click **Quickwords**.

2) Select the abbreviated form.
   Click **Insert in text**.

Using the Keyboard to Retrieve an Abbreviation

1) Type the name of the abbreviation, e.g. Thank1.

2) Press the **<spacebar>** on the keyboard.

Mail Merge - I

What is Mail Merge?

Mail Merge enables you to combine a standard (*Form*) letter with a file of names and addresses, thus producing, simply and quickly, a batch of personalised letters.

The Stages

There are three stages to performing a Mail Merge. The details of how to execute each one are given in the next few pages.

1) The first stage is to create a datafile. This will usually be a file of names and addresses.

2)
```
1st February 1998

FIELD(Company)
FIELD(Street)
FIELD(Town)
FIELD(County)

Dear Sirs,

Please find enclosed...
```
The second stage is to create a standard letter. Wherever a piece of personalised information is to appear, you insert a field heading.

3) The third stage is to combine the standard letter with the datafile to produce personalised documents.

```
1st February 1998

Jones Ltd
6 High Street
Brighton
Sussex

Dear Sirs,

Please find enclosed...
```

```
1st February 1998

Short Ltd
9 Shore Hill
Hove
Sussex

Dear Sirs,

Please find enclosed...
```

```
1st February 1998

Browns Ltd
6 Skylarks
Crawley
Sussex

Dear Sirs,

Please find enclosed...
```

Mail Merge - II

Creating your DataFile

1) Click **Tools**, click **Merge**, click **Create Data**.

2) You now need to decide on the field headings that you require. A typical datafile might consist of the following fields.

> COMPANY - To store the name of the company.
> STREET - To store the first line of their address.
> TOWN - To store the name of the town that they are in.
> COUNTY - To store the names of the county they are in.
> POSTCODE - To store their postcode.

Type the first field heading COMPANY in the **Name a Field**.
Click **Add** to confirm it.

Enter all the rest of the headings in this way.
Click **OK**.

3) You are now in the *Quick Data Entry Form.*
Enter the details of your customers. Use the **<Enter>** key on the keyboard to confirm each entry and take you to the next box. Press the **<Enter>** key on the last field and a new blank form will come into view.

4) When you have entered the last address, click **Close**.

5) Click **Yes** to save your changes to disk. Give your data file a name in the **File name** box and click **Save**.

6) Click **File**, click **Close**.

Mail Merge - III

Creating the Standard Letter

1) Click **Tools**, click **Merge**.

2) Click **Create Document**.

3) Select your datafile by clicking the icon to the right of the **Associate a Data File** box. Choose your datafile from the list. Click **Select**. Click **OK**.

4) You should now be able to see the merge button bar on the screen. The button on the far left hand side of it looks like this.

Type your standard letter. Whenever you want to put in one of the fields from your datafile, click the **Insert Field** button.

5) After you have clicked the Insert Field button, a list of fields will pop up.

    Select the one that you want.

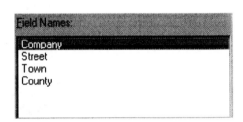

6) Click the Insert button.

7) The field name will appear in your document.

FIELD(Company)

Merging the Standard Letter with the Data File

1) With the standard letter still open, click the **Merge** button.

2) Click **Merge**.